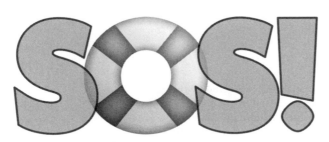

A Practical Guide for Leading Solution-Focused Groups with Kids K–12

Patricia K. Tollison
Katherine O. Synatschk

Illustrations by Christine Synatschk

pro·ed
An International Publisher

8700 Shoal Creek Boulevard
Austin, Texas 78757-6897
800/897-3202 Fax 800/397-7633
www.proedinc.com

Art Director: Jason Crosier
Designer: Nancy McKinney
This book is designed in FairfieldLH, Agenda, and AshleyScriptMT.

Printed in the United States of America

1 2 3 4 5 6 7 8 9 10   10 09 08 07 06

To Mark, Sarah Jane, Zack, and Katie

To Martin, Matthew, Joseph, Susan, and Katie

Contents

PART 1

SOS Groups: The Structure   1

Chapter 8
SOS Group Lesson Plans and Activities   113

Preface

"Harry—yer a wizard."

"I'm a what?" gasped Harry.

"A wizard, o' course," said Hagrid... "an' a thumpin' good'un, I'd say, once yeh've been trained up a bit."

—J. K. Rowling, *Harry Potter and the Sorcerer's Stone*

We believe in the value of group counseling for kids. We are aware that creating a group program can seem like a daunting task in any setting, schools included. Counselors and other mental health professionals in schools face the daily challenges of limited time and great demand for service. Groups would seem the answer to at least part of the problem. Yet the old saying "It's hard to remember that you're clearing the swamp when you're up to your (shall we say) waist in alligators" comes to mind. Planning and setting up groups can often seem like tall orders and several more items on a very long list.

We wrote this book in response to these concerns and with the intention of helping busy professionals in schools take the leap over the hurdles of creating new or expanding current group programs. This book presents a foundation for group work and a guide for developing effective and efficient groups. Although the discussion is based in educational settings, the practical approach we describe need not be limited to that context. It is our hope that helpers who work with young people in other settings will be able to adapt these practical ideas to meet their unique needs.

The group work model presented in this book addresses counselors' need for efficient use of time; the need for students to gain skills to advance personally, socially, and academically; and the need for schools to take a positive, strengths-based approach to students' needs. This group model is specifically aimed at something we believe all students need to succeed: a strengthened sense of self. Thus the name of our model became Strengthening Sense of Self, or SOS. The SOS model takes the foundation of group work with all its benefits and adds solution-focused approaches in combination with psychoeducational content. This model calls on the personal resources of group members in a structured setting that teaches kids to have strengths-based dialogues with themselves and others and teaches new skills each time they meet as a group. The goal is for students to help themselves and each other to become increasingly competent in handling the challenges that come their way.

This is a group work model that is positive *and* versatile. Each kid in an SOS group can work on a different referral issue while all the members learn the skills that they need to know to grow into successful adults. The structure is well defined and easy to manage. The result is that many more kids can participate in groups during the school year, with no need for the counselor to create an array of topical groups.

In many respects this is a "how to" book. We assume that the reader has had basic instruction in group counseling, but we offer numerous opportunities to expand and develop skills through exercises, tips, and examples. Brief vignettes help illustrate concepts and hopefully enrich your reading experience. The book is divided into eight chapters. In the first three chapters we present a discussion of the benefits of group counseling, what the SOS model includes, and how to successfully use SOS group leadership skills. In Chapters 4 through 6 we describe the practical aspects of establishing groups in schools, how to get kids ready to participate in your SOS groups, and what the sessions look like when the model is implemented. Chapter 7 comes complete with scripts and detailed plans for the sessions and will enable you to facilitate the six-session unit. Chapter 8 includes group activities and reproducibles in the six content areas for primary, intermediate, and secondary levels. There are three levels of activities of increasing difficulty in each age group—for a total of fifty-four group activities—to provide the foundation for the psychoeducational portion of each group session. Additionally, the reproducibles are available on the enclosed CD-ROM.

There is a critical need for kids in schools to receive excellent counseling to assist them in meeting their challenges. Counselors are continually disheartened by the difficulties in reaching all of the students in their care. The SOS model offers hope for counselors and kids. Counselors are provided with a carefully defined program that offers students the benefits of group work and the opportunity to learn new skills, to find their own solutions and meet their goals, and to leave the group with a stronger sense of self. We began this project with enthusiasm, and this enthusiasm has carried us through with the belief that we are offering you and the kids you work with an innovative and energizing approach to group work. We wish you a fulfilling future of SOS groups!

Patricia Tollison, PhD
Katherine Synatschk, PhD, LPC

Acknowledgments

From Patricia K. Tollison

I want to thank Glenn Hirsch, who introduced me to the discipline and art of group leadership. I am deeply indebted to him and to my earliest co-therapists, Tony Arden and Alan Boyd (deceased).

Much of what I know about the true benefits of group relationships I learned first-hand through Scott Rutan's leadership and with my fellow members of his Austin training group. I thank him and each of them, along with the larger Austin group therapy community, whose enthusiasm and curiosity continue to inspire me to grow professionally and personally.

I am indebted to Bill Bruzy, who introduced me to PRO-ED, and to Kate Adams, Joanne Olsen, and Joan Ranson for their ideas and support of my work on this book.

Finally, I want to especially acknowledge the members of the groups I have led during the past twenty-five years. They have been my most benevolent teachers.

From Kathy O. Synatschk

I want to thank the counselors of the Austin Independent School District, whose dedication and fine work with students inspired my desire to create a tool to bring together all of the best aspects of solution-focused counseling approaches with psychoeducational groups. I appreciate, also, my teachers of Solution-Focused Therapy— Insoo Kim Berg, Bill O'Hanlon, John Murphy, Linda Metcalf, and Willyn Webb—whose valuable work continues to improve the lives of so many. Most of all, I want to thank all of the students I have had the privilege to work with and who allowed me to share in their growth through many challenges and triumphs. They taught me the value of accepting and embracing their views and their own creative ideas for solutions.

List of Primary-Level Group Topics with Objectives and Activities (Grades K–3)

Topic Area	Title	Objectives	Activities
		Group members will:	
Self-Knowledge and Acceptance	Discovery Hunt	get to know other group members and recognize that there is something unique about everyone	Discovery Hunt
	Identify Your Feelings	identify their own feelings as they occur	Identify Your Feelings situation cards
	Showing Your Feelings	identify feelings and choose how and when to express them	Feelings poster, lists of feelings, and Showing Your Feelings situation cards
Interpersonal and Communication Skills	Formulating I–Statements	practice expressing their thoughts, feelings, and wants effectively	Getting Your Message Across
	How To Recognize a Good Listener	recognize and demonstrate the skills of good listening	How to Recognize a Good Listener Experience Sheet
	Name Game	identify ways to compliment others and plan to compliment a specific person	Warm Fuzzy and Friendship Wheel
Responsible Behavior	Accepting Responsibility Versus Blaming Others	be able to accept responsibility for their actions without blaming others	Accepting Responsibility poster, Responsibility cards, Choosing the Best Response page
	Welcome to Manners Land!	determine whether manners are being used in various situations and demonstrate the use of appropriate, respectful manners in simulated situations	Manners Land cards
	Something I've Done to Improve Our World	describe ways in which they can be responsible for contributing to the betterment of their community or world	Improving Our World cards

Topic Area	Title	Objectives	Activities
Conflict Resolution	The Turtle Technique for Tempering Anger	use a visualization technique to help inhibit negative behavior when angry	The Turtle Trick poster, 1–2–3–Turtle!, Turtle Power!
	Using Refusal Skills	learn effective methods for saying "no" and practice refusal skills by role-playing actual situations	The Cool Kid's Guide to Saying "No" sheet, Refusal cards
	Expressing Your Anger	express anger without hitting	Expressing Your Anger sheet, Anger cards
Decision Making	Consequences of Choices and Decisions	learn that there are consequences for poor choices and decisions	Consequences of Choices and Decisions poster, Problem cards
	Goal Wheel	identify a goal and describe what to do each day during the week to reach the goal	Goal Wheel
	Overcoming Obstacles to Goals	identify a goal, describe possible obstacles to reaching the goal, and make a plan to overcome the obstacles	Climbing High contract
Self-Care	Relaxing	use relaxation techniques when needed	Relaxing poster and Relaxation Technique poster
	Affirm Your Body!	discuss body images as a way to improve them, build a more positive relationship with their physical selves, celebrate their positive physical qualities, and create an artistic model of their bodies	Butcher paper art activity
	My Body and Me	experience the practice of self-massage, practice a set of movements for stress relief, become aware of the body, and celebrate the self in the body	Massage activity

List of Intermediate-Level Group Topics with Objectives and Activities (Grades 4–7)

Topic Area	Title	Objectives	Activities
		Group members will:	
Self-Knowledge and Acceptance	Getting to Know You and Me	share information about themselves and learn about their group members	Discussion cards, Getting to Know You and Me sharing cards
	"WANTED"	identify their unique qualities, strengths, and special talents; share these talents with the group, and learn those of the group	"WANTED" poster activity
	How We See Ourselves: Self-Assessment, Sharing, and Discussion	rate the degree to which they possess specific qualities, represent their self-concept pictorially or in words, and describe how self-concept affects daily living	Looking at Me Self-Assessment
Interpersonal and Communication Skills	I–Messages: Still No Substitute!	describe how they typically handle negative feelings in conflict situations, practice formulating and delivering I–messages, and state the benefits of I–messages over other ways of handling negative feelings	I–Messages cards
	The Active Listener	define the role of the receiver in communication and identify and demonstrate "active listening" behaviors	Communication Process diagram, topic cards, The Active Listener poster
	The Clique Phenomenon	identify ways to make new friends, define the term clique, describe the effects of cliques, and state how they can avoid making other people feel left out	Making New Friends poster, Getting on Your Own Side

Topic Area	Title	Objectives	Activities
Responsible Behavior	Steps for Solving a Problem Responsibly	develop and practice a process for effective problem solving	Steps for Solving a Problem Responsibly activity
	Manners Land: Intermediate	determine whether manners are being used in various situations and demonstrate the use of appropriate, respectful manners	Manners Land cards
	Have to … Choose to …	contrast the attitude of being compelled to do something with the attitude of choosing to do it; describe the feelings associated with taking responsibility for their actions	Have to … Choose to … Experience Sheet
Conflict Resolution	Exploring Alternatives to Conflict	learn and practice specific strategies for resolving conflict	Conflict Resolution Strategies sheet
	Up and Down Escalators: Raising and Lowering the Level of Conflict	identify behaviors that escalate and de-escalate conflict; practice using communication skills to control the escalation of conflicts	Up and Down Escalators scenarios
	What Am I Thinking?	identify how unclear communication can lead to conflict and describe ways communication can be made clear to prevent misunderstandings	Balloon activity
Decision Making	Decisions, Decisions!	understand and describe how decisions are influenced and develop and practice a process for effective decision making	Decision-Making Process poster, Decision-Making Process cards
	Setting and Attaining Goals	explain that having a goal is the first step to achieving what one wants, identify specific steps for attaining goals, develop skills in setting practical and achievable goals, and experience goal attainment	Tips for Setting Goals sheet, Goal Achievement Score sheet
	Decisions and Outcomes	understand and describe how decisions are influenced by many factors, and state the outcomes and possible consequences of specific decisions	More About Decisions handout, Decision Discussion cards
Self-Care	The Breath of Life	learn and practice two deep-breathing exercises and identify times when they can use these exercises for relaxation and renewal	Deep-breathing exercises
	S–T–O–P That Thought	learn a model for halting negative thinking patterns, practice the model, brainstorm recurring thoughts they would like to stop, and decide on a specific thought pattern to S–T–O–P in daily life	S–T–O–P That Thought model activity
	The Memory Poem	recall poignant memories, reflect and write about the memories, share poetry and memories, and discuss the process of releasing memories	Memory Poem worksheet

List of Secondary-Level Group Topics with Objectives and Activities (Grades 8–12)

Topic Area	Title	Objectives	Activities
		Group members will:	
Self-Knowledge and Acceptance	Something About Me You Wouldn't Know Unless I Told You	share something about themselves that is neither obvious nor generally known and describe what it feels like to disclose information about themselves	Something About Me Discussion cards
	How We See Ourselves	rate the degree to which they possess specific qualities or characteristics, represent their self-concept pictorially or in words, and describe how self-concept affects daily living	Looking at Me Self-Assessment handout
	Who Am I?	identify likes and dislikes and areas of strength and weakness, clarify personal values, and explain how self-awareness facilitates performance	Who Am I? handout
Interpersonal and Communication Skills	The Assert Formula	identify their rights in interpersonal situations, identify ways to communicate assertively using oral and nonverbal language, and practice making I–statements	Student Bill of Rights poster, Watch Your Body Language poster, Assert Formula cards
	Mastering Assertive Communication	describe the differences between assertive, aggressive, and passive behaviors; practice assertive and nonassertive behaviors in role-play situations; and explain how assertive, aggressive, and passive behaviors affect situations involving harassment	Communication Styles poster, Acting Assertively scenario cards
	Group Discussion Roles	develop listening and speaking skills to enhance communication	Group Discussion Roles poster, role cards, Leader Issue Scenario cards

Topic Area	Title	Objectives	Activities
Responsible Behavior	Improving the Study Habit	learn and practice effective study habits and develop and implement plans for self-improvement	Study Skills Assessment, Study Skills and Habits poster
	Freedom and Responsibility	define what is responsible behavior in three situations and discuss the meaning of freedom and its relationship to responsibility	Writing activity
	Who's in Charge?	recognize the degree of personal control over events	Who's in Charge? sheet
Conflict Resolution	Assessing Anger Styles	identify two recent events that caused them to feel angry and describe what they did in each situation, assess the effectiveness of their typical behaviors when angry, examine and discuss several common anger styles, and explain how they can choose more effective responses in situations that provoke anger	Assessing Your Anger sheet, Anger Styles poster
	Problem Solving: The Win–Win Strategy	examine a win–win problem-solving process and discuss its benefits and practice using problem solving to resolve specific conflicts	Getting to Win–Win sheet
	Managing Moods	explain how moods are affected by feelings left over from conflicts, identify problems and feelings associated with specific conflicts, and describe strategies for releasing residual feelings and managing negative moods	Lousy Moods cards
Decision Making	Decisions, Decisions!	understand and describe how decisions are influenced and develop and practice a process for effective decision making	The Decision-Making Process sheet
	Approval and Consequences	recognize the advantages and disadvantages of doing something to gain social approval	Approval and Consequences cards
	Looking Back on a Decision I Made	describe and evaluate decisions they have made	Decisions cards
Self-Care	Success Bombardment	recognize and describe their own worth and worthiness; identify strengths, talents, and special abilities in themselves and others; and practice positive self-talk	Success Inventory, Target worksheet
	Centering and Balancing	identify and label stressful situations associated with strong negative emotions and practice a simple meditation exercise that can be used to relieve stress and regain emotional balance	Meditation exercise
	Effectively Managing Time	keep track of their time use for one week and identify specific ways of organizing their time and surroundings	Keeping a Time Log sheet, Time Management Tips

Part 1

SOS Groups:
The Structure

1

Choosing to Work with Groups

What Makes Group Work Different?

Specific Benefits

The Meaning of a Strengthened Sense of Self

We define a group as three or more kids, who are peers and who meet on a regular basis with a counselor for psychological and educational purposes. Studies have shown that peer relationships are predictive of mental health (Kymissis & Halperin, 1996), and peer groups provide unique opportunities for children and adolescents to learn and practice skills that improve their peer relationships. Group counseling shares similarities with individual counseling, such as a focus on kids' growth and change, but is different in some specific ways (Malekoff, 2004).

What Makes Group Work Different?

Group work is different than individual counseling. Group work's unique characteristics include:

- In a group we have the opportunity to experience children in active relationships with us and with their peers simultaneously.
- Group leaders get to observe an individual kid's reactions to others in the room and to the group leaders.
- These observations are used to improve the student's ability to interact more productively with others and to internalize more positive views in relationship to authority and peers.
- The group creates a "family" that has the express purpose of encouraging each member to grow and change.
- Group experience mirrors real life in ways that individual counseling cannot. Our experiences with the students are more like the experiences of their teachers. Kids have to share attention, take turns, and listen to others. The kids have their problems right in the room with their peers and with you.

- When we work individually with students, we are talking about difficulties in the abstract. For example, the child who feels left out by others comes to an individual session and talks about the problem. In a group, however, this kid will experience the difficulty in real time (not in the abstract) and we can help him or her solve the problem as it occurs.

- In group, the student will not be excluded and will have the opportunity to practice new behaviors with help (Swanson, 1996).

- We invite the whole kid to come to the meetings (Malekoff, 2004). The aggressive kid is aggressive; the distractible kid is distracted. As leaders of groups we can see in action the available strengths and the areas for improvement. The aggressive kid may have a good sense of humor and the distractible kid may have a creative mind.

- The whole child includes the part that has strengths and the internal resources to solve his or her problems and the part that is having difficulty.

Specific Benefits

The professional literature suggests that group counseling is helpful to students (Whiston & Sexton, 1998), and group counseling offers many benefits in the school setting. In order to promote and organize groups effectively, we have to be sold on their unique benefits (Malekoff, 2004).

Economy

We want to sell you on groups, so we will start with the undeniable benefit that in a group we see a number of students at the same time (Yalom & Leszcz, 2005). Instead of spending thirty minutes or an hour with one child, we work with three to eight children in the same time period. We get "face time" with more kids.

Group sometimes has been thought of as a second-best option, chosen primarily because of the economy involved. For many kids, being a part of a group has more rapid, direct carryover to their everyday lives than does individual counseling. We suggest this carryover occurs through the therapeutic use of the varied relationships in the group. Economy is always an important consideration, but the fact remains that group would be the best counseling choice for many kids even if it were more "expensive."

Mutual Support

You are not alone with students' presenting problems and neither are the group members. Members get to have the experience of helping others and being helped by others in specific ways (Rutan & Stone, 2001). Through productive self-expression and feedback, members get help with the problems that brought them to groups. Each time they make use of help or are helpful to another member, there is the potential for their improvement of their sense of mastery. They have witnesses to their efforts and progress.

A great deal of what we believe is helpful about being a part of a group has to do with having new experiences with receiving and giving attention. It is our belief that being given attention by others and sharing attention in a healthy way lead to a strengthened sense of self. In any group, altruism can develop as kids give and receive help (Malekoff, 2004).

Universality

Group work gives members the immediate experience that others have problems also (Yalom & Leszcz, 2005). The sense of "We're all in the same boat here" is a relief. Hearing that other kids need help with solving their problems provides members with the opportunity to be empathic with one another and sympathetic with themselves.

Instillation of Hope

Having hope suggests the expectation that what we want to happen is likely to happen. The message of hope is "We're working together and we know this will help." At any given time individual members will be at different stages as they work toward their goals. The member who has made progress and speaks specifically about that progress offers hope to those who have not made progress (Rutan & Stone, 2001; Yalom & Leszcz, 2005). As leaders, we have the ongoing opportunity to instill hope when we notice progress and to compliment effort.

Social Learning

A group is a social experience. Members are expected to take turns, to share center stage, to take their fair share of time, and, in general, to act in ways that demonstrate respect for others. They do not do this perfectly. The group work experience offers kids the chance to practice, make mistakes, and learn from those mistakes through the experience itself and through constructive feedback (Malekoff, 2004). Groups are a microcosm of society and as such provide real-life settings in which students can work out issues and problems (Brigman & Early, 1991; Gladding, 2003).

Kids frequently get helpful feedback from adults. If the feedback is too frequent, they often tune us out. Feedback from peers that is not derogatory and hurtful is the rare commodity that a group offers. As leaders, our job is to create the environment that makes it possible for members to interact constructively with one another and to experience a sense of cohesiveness with their peers.

Experiencing Healthy Self-Expression

With the shared purpose of solving problems, members of groups are given the opportunity to be listened to and helped in an encouraging environment. In groups, members can give expression to their feelings, their ideas, their life experiences, and their hopes and dreams. Acceptance, clear boundaries, and clarity of purpose creates a "family" where there are opportunities for members to have what has been called a "corrective relational experience" (Rutan & Stone, 2001).

Developing Knowledge and Skills

In this book we introduce a specific model for running groups in school settings. We call these groups Strengthening Sense of Self (SOS) groups. They are designed to help kindergarten through twelfth-grade students with a variety of presenting problems.

In SOS groups we teach members how to use the solution-focused approach to change. Solution-focused counseling is based on the idea that change occurs when individuals define their problems in their own words, take ownership of the problems, and use their strengths to set and meet goals. Students learn to use the approach to help themselves and to help one another with the problems that bring them to group. They learn from one another's experiences. There is a psychoeducational component in the SOS group model designed to educate kids in six core content areas for their use in meeting their goals. All children, regardless of their presenting issues, benefit from learning skills in the six areas. Through the group experience, members have opportunities to learn empathy and cooperation at meetings and have a safe arena in which to try out new skills and behaviors. As leaders we organize the experience so that the group rewards progress toward members' goals and toward greater self-reliance.

Summary of Specific Benefits of Group Work

- Groups offer contact with more students in the same time period. Frequently there is positive change that has more rapid, direct carryover to everyday life.

- Group provides the experience of peer support for positive change. Students learn to give attention to and share attention with peers.

- The student learns that others have similar experiences.

- The group holds the expectation that members can make positive changes.

- Group membership offers direct opportunities to improve peer relationships and relationships with adults. Members can receive constructive feedback from peers.

- The group experience encourages improved self-expression in members.

- Strengthening Sense of Self groups help students with a variety of presenting problems. These groups teach members a set of skills to improve their abilities to create solutions to their problems.

The Meaning of a Strengthened Sense of Self

The unique benefit of being a part of a well-organized counseling group is that it helps kids' sense of self. This is true for the student whose presenting problem is a transient one as well as for the student with ongoing difficulties.

Defining a Sense of Self

Kymissis and Halperin (1996) described the sense of self "not as a passive recipient, but an active doer" (p. 24). They stated that before approximately age seven the young child's sense of self is defined as "I am what I will be," shifting around age seven to "I am what I learn." After approximately age twelve, moving into adolescence, an individual's sense of self is strongly affected by status with peers and the need to give and receive love.

"The person who is me, who is only me," is the way that D. W. Winnicott (1971, p. ix), a masterful clinician who did pioneering work with children and adolescents, described the self. We speak of the self here as the sum of the internal pictures we carry of our self and important others in our lives. A sense of self also includes the feelings we have about these pictures and how they guide our capacity to act in our environment (Masterson, 1988).

By kindergarten our sense of self carries at least some subjective experience in regard to: *Who do I like? Who likes me? What do I do well? What is hard for me? What can I expect from others? What do others expect from me? What is the likelihood that I will succeed by my own effort?* Each kid is different and the internal, mostly unarticulated answers students carry to these questions have a profound effect on behavior. Thinking of each student in terms of his or her sense of self helps us to respond to each individual more effectively.

A Strengthened Sense of Self

The following list has been adapted from James F. Masterson's book *The Search for the Real Self* (1988). As you consider this list, keep in mind that all of us, especially kids, are "works in progress." This list represents what we might expect from a sense of self that has been strengthened through life experience.

- Expression of both positive and negative feelings that seem predictable and age-appropriate in response to life events.
- Expectation that we can accomplish what we set out to do, that we will be rewarded for our efforts, and that we will receive a positive response from others.
- Ability to take action on our own behalf, such as asking for help.
- Realistic acknowledgment of our skills and abilities and acceptance of new information about ourselves, our skills, and our abilities.
- Acknowledgment and soothing of our own painful feelings as well as acceptance of support from others.
- Making and sticking with commitments to ourselves and to others.
- Finding new ways to deal with problems and learn from mistakes.
- Making and maintaining friendships, forming productive relationships with important others in our lives, and making use of feedback that we get from others about our impacts on them.

- Ability to be emotionally independent at an age-appropriate level, keeping in mind the concern of others for us even when they are not immediately available, or when there is conflict.
- Maintenance of our sense of self when things go well and when things do not go well.

Reading through the list above, an image of kids with strengthened sense of self emerges. What also emerges is the image of kids who do not have that strong sense of self. Students in the latter group

- may have difficulty when their needs come into conflict with the needs of others, creating interpersonal problems.
- may have unrealistic expectations about their abilities to succeed.
- may have so much interpersonal anxiety that they panic and act out.
- may not accept personal responsibility.
- may not experience themselves as emotionally independent and may not maintain healthy interpersonal boundaries.
- may struggle to attain a strengthened sense of self.

SOS groups provide an environment specifically designed to teach kids to set their own goals and to support their active roles in making changes. Group members have the direct opportunity to improve interpersonal relationships through the experiences of giving and receiving help and constructive feedback. They also have the opportunity to internalize the concern of others and to leave with a strengthened sense of self.

Summary

- Groups include three or more members, so you can help more than one individual at a time.
- Having to share time and attention in a group mirrors real life and has more rapid, direct carryover to students' lives outside than does individual counseling.
- Group work uses relationships in the room for growth and change by creating positive "families."
- As a group leader you can observe the kids' strengths and difficulties in the group room.
- Groups have many benefits that include the offer of hope and the awareness that we are not alone; opportunities to give and receive support, to share attention, and to learn healthy self-expression; and opportunities to acquire new information and to develop new skills.
- SOS groups teach and use the solution-focused counseling approach, and have a psychoeducational component. The SOS

model can be used with students with different presenting problems from kindergarten through twelfth grade.

- Group work is uniquely suited to strengthening senses of self.
- The sense of self, in large part, defines relationships to others and interactions with others. The sense of self is directly related to our perception of our ability to succeed, and this sense of self guides our capacity to act on our own behalf.

2 Learning the SOS Group Model

Overview of the SOS Group Model

The solution-focused SOS group model is specifically designed to help students in school settings. We use the letters "SOS" to refer to Strengthened Sense of Self. The letters SOS are also associated with an emergency call for help, which is directly related to the fact that some members are referred to SOS groups because of a life crisis. Others are referred simply for help in making positive changes.

The SOS group model brings together the benefits of group, solution-focused, and psychoeducational counseling approaches. It is a group model that we can describe with confidence when we communicate with colleagues and parents. SOS groups are organized in brief, six-session units. Usually these groups meet weekly for six weeks with the option of recontracting for additional six-session units. We encourage the use of a "booster" session, or sessions, after the group has ended to help support the progress that members made. The amount of time between graduation and booster session is determined by the unique needs of each group.

An initial solution-focused interview is held with each potential member to determine if an SOS group would meet this particular student's needs. During the interview we begin teaching students to use the solution-focused approach by working with them to define problems and to establish clear, achievable goals. If we determine (with the kids' input) that being in a group is a good decision, the goals go with them into group. This initial interview begins to instill hope and demonstrates respect for the kid's ability to be responsible through the message, "You can define your problem and create a plan for change for yourself."

From the first SOS group meeting to the group graduation, meetings begin with a progress check-in. A group culture is established that lets members know they are together to help one another meet their goals. Members are asked to talk about how their individual plans have worked during the week. Early goals are accomplished, new goals are set, and difficulties are addressed using the solution-focused approach. Members' growth and change are also supported through the use of psychoeducational activities to develop specific skills.

A concern we often hear about groups is that kids may learn new ways to misbehave. It is true that in a group, kids hear other kids talk about their difficulties. However, the solution-focused approach sets SOS groups apart from other groups. As the leader maintains solution-focused group conversation, members are given the rich experience of hearing one another's problems and then becoming involved in creating solutions. Members have the direct experience of helping themselves and others meet goals and set new goals, giving them the opportunity to feel useful and valuable to one another. The message is "We all have problems and we all can succeed!"

Effective use of the group and the combination of the solution-focused and psychoeducational processes make it possible for many members to experience a sense of mastery in areas of their lives where they have previously not felt successful. Observe the experiences of a group member in the following example.

A GROUP PRACTICING I–STATEMENTS

A fourth-grade group of six members meeting for the second time was addressing a conflict issue. Two members, Don and Barry, shared the goal of improving their ability to control their anger. At check-in the leader heard that during the week Don had difficulty with his goal of remembering to count to ten when he felt angry, while Barry had more success. The psychoeducational content activity for this meeting was to learn how to use and to practice using I–Statements when speaking to someone who had upset them.

The leader chose Barry to first role-play a person who was very upset and let Don be the person who stayed calm and used I–Statements. Then she had them reverse roles. Afterward, Don reported to the group that he had a really hard time staying upset when it was his turn to do so. He said it felt so much better to be the one who stayed calm. Barry reported that he didn't like being the "angry one" either. Both members got positive feedback for the efforts they had made. The leader amplified members' experience by asking how they could use this new understanding the next time they were upset.

Don had a new, positive experience with mastery. Help for him came through the use of the psychoeducational activity. He was taught to use thinking to control his impulses. This example also illustrates the leader's use of the value of being a part of a group. Through the skill development activity she created the opportunity for Don and Barry to experience the leader's and the group's support.

Making Use of a Problem

Group experiences do not always go as planned, however. How could the model have been used if the leader had faced a different situation?

In the role-play activity, if Don were unable to stick with the I–Statements, the SOS group leader would have had a variety of options. One would be to tell Don that this would be a good time to get some help from other members. Then, thinking of an example in her own mind while looking to the whole group, she could ask who remembered a time in this role play when Don did use an I–Statement well. If group members responded, the leader could explain the example. If no group members responded, the leader could give the example she remembered, or help the group and Don remember with some prompting. She might then ask how he was able to use the I–Statement at one point and encourage other group members to talk about similar experiences.

Even when things do not go smoothly when we lead SOS groups, we can use those moments to provide a member, a few members, or the whole group with the experience of a healthy "family" responding to difficulties. The use of the content areas and the solution-focused process provide ongoing opportunities for the group and the leader to mirror the strengths of each member. With consistency and repeated experiences of setting goals and being acknowledged for their improvement, members of SOS groups begin to see themselves the way they are seen in the group. Members leave group with a greater sense of self-efficacy.

SOS groups bring together group, solution-focused, and psychoeducational counseling approaches to provide a strong foundation for leading groups in schools. In the following sections we describe how SOS groups make use of each of these three theoretical frameworks.

The Group Counseling Approach

As leaders of groups, we shift our thinking from the way we work with individuals to how to make best use of all this help we now have. Making use of members' abilities to help one another is an essential group leadership skill. A common concern of adult potential group members is that they do not want to listen to other members' problems. This concern may stem from a lack of confidence about their ability to be helpful to others. Groups are natural settings for kids (Swanson, 1996), who do not share this adult concern. We have only to provide a safe place and the opportunity to speak for kids to get busy helping one another.

In SOS groups we encourage enough storytelling by members for them to get to know one another, but we are careful to protect members from sharing what would be harmful to them. Our task is to redirect conversation to members' goals and their strengths. This sometimes requires us to block members from sharing intimate family information, inviting them to speak to us about that in private. It also requires us to block nonproductive, negative feedback or nonproductive confrontation between members.

Group members often listen more carefully and receive feedback more easily from one another than from us. This is hard to remember. Our job is to facilitate productive conversation between members. We do this by maintaining the boundaries and by providing consistency and structure in the group. Within the predictable group structure, we encourage members to look to themselves and to one another rather than to us for answers. Sometimes we do this by pointing out how another member has faced that same difficulty, noting the similarities; or we might ask that the other member give some information about an experience with a similar problem. Depending on the maturity level of the group, we might encourage members to speak spontaneously when they have an idea they think would be helpful. As leaders of SOS groups we are always giving the group and each member the message that through their owns efforts and by helping one another, they can solve their problems. The following vignette illustrates a leader facilitating goal-directed interaction.

The leader of a seventh-grade SOS group was meeting with the group for the fifth time. A group member, Lisa, expressed disappointment with herself because she had not been able to stick with her goal of doing her assigned math homework each day right after school. Lisa looked to the leader and said, "I don't think I'll ever be able to do math and I don't want to anyway."

The leader felt the pull to try to solve this problem for Lisa, knowing how difficult Lisa's life was at home. Taking a breath, the leader made eye contact with Lisa and acknowledged Lisa's disappointment. The leader then turned to another group member, Leticia, whose home environment was similar to Lisa's, and said, "Leticia, I'm thinking you are one of the experts in this group about the problem Lisa is having with her math goal. What is one thing you know she can do to help herself?"

Leticia smiled at Lisa and said, "Girl, you need to give yourself a break. I remember seeing you do your math last week while we were waiting for the bus in the cafeteria."

The leader made a careful choice in enlisting Leticia's help in this example. She resisted the position that she was the only one in the room who could help Lisa and, instead, empowered Leticia and the group to help one another. Leticia's effort also illustrates the use of exceptions (those circumstances in which the problem does not occur, or occurs less often or less intensely) to support change.

Group Development

A group and its members need time and experiences to develop trust in one another. In the seventh-grade group described above, members had been in the group long enough for the leader to encourage risk taking between members. Even in brief groups like SOS groups, trust needs time to develop. The group leader's job is to be aware of this and not push members to take risks too quickly. We facilitate trust through managing the boundaries carefully, by demonstrating our respect for ideas expressed in the group, and by blocking nonproductive interaction.

As trust develops in the group, we often see members taking the risk of differing opinions and expressing more displeasure with the group when we ask for feedback. Members may decide they do not want to come to the group anymore. When this happens, we have to call on our own confidence in the group process and remind ourselves that this is a normal part of a group's development. The most helpful stance we can take is to listen, maintain the boundaries, and continue to direct the group back to its work.

Every time group members weather a developmental storm, they are in a much stronger position to work together as a cohesive unit. We have sent the message that we can listen to negative feelings and differences of opinion and continue to work together. Of equal importance in an SOS group is that none of the disturbance distracts us from the purpose of working together toward our goals.

The reality that the group will end soon often becomes a regular part of the conversation. SOS groups are brief groups, and members often begin talking about the group ending at the first meeting. Leaders have a responsibility to pay attention to how members talk about this topic and to bring the topic up in the last few meetings if members do not. This responsibility helps members to say good-bye to this experience, plan for continuing work on their goals, and make new goals.

The Solution-Focused Counseling Approach

Solution-focused counseling offers great promise as a time-effective, cooperative approach that shifts the counselor's focus from "what's wrong" to "what's working" with students. The beliefs, resources, and competencies of kids, parents, and teachers are actively sought and applied to the resolution of school problems (Murphy, 1997). The solution-focused counseling approach addresses the counseling relationship, collaboration in goal setting, and ongoing evaluation of progress.

Establishing Working Relationships

When kids are referred for group or we see that group would be an effective intervention, we meet with them for an initial interview. John Murphy, in his helpful book *Solution-Focused Counseling in Middle and High Schools* (1997), wisely emphasizes taking a respectful and curious stance towards kids' perceptions of what brings them to our offices for a first interview. We move out of the position that we are the ones with all the answers. Watchful of any tendency to impose our own views of the problem, we build rapport and work to understand the problem as the child sees it. This shift in our thinking and communication takes conscious effort and practice. Our effort will continue to pay off as we communicate from the beginning that the student has all the resources it will take to solve this personal problem.

It is important to listen carefully to the student's story. We want to listen particularly to the use of language and for indications of where we can identify strengths. At the end of the story we will be looking for what this kid wants to change in the situation. Clearly, kids do not have the power to change much about their life circumstances, but what they *can* change are the ways they are acting and reacting that cause difficulties.

Collaboration and Goal Setting

Once we have an understanding of the student's perception of what needs to be changed, we use this information and the kid's own language as much as possible to define the problem. The more clearly and specifically the problem is stated, the easier it will be to develop behavioral goals for change.

Goal setting is a key process because we want to assist with setting goals and simultaneously teach the goal-setting process. Younger students may need quite a bit of assistance and suggestions from us; middle school and high school students are best given as much independence in the process as possible.

TABLE 2.1

Characteristics of Effective Goals

Characteristic	Description	Useful Questions
Specific	Clear, concrete, specific, observable	"What will you be doing differently when you have 'higher self-esteem'?"
		"What kind of things will be different when things start improving?"
Small	Modest, realistic, reasonable, attainable	"What will be the first small sign that things are getting better at school?"
		"You said that things in math class were at a 4 on a scale of 1 to 10. What will a 5 look like?"
Positive	Stated as the presence of something desirable rather than the absence of something undesirable	"What will you be doing *instead of* being depressed?"
		"What should this student be doing *instead of* goofing off?"
Meaningful	Relevant and important to the client	"What do you want to accomplish in counseling?"
		What do you think is the most important thing we need to change in this situation?"

Note. From *Solution-Focused Counseling in Middle and High Schools,* by J. J. Murphy, 1997, p. 75. Copyright 1997 by the American Counseling Association. Used with permission.

Teaching the solution-focused process is an integral aspect of SOS groups. Murphy (1997) outlined the characteristics of effective goals, which are described in Table 2.1.

After the goals are set satisfactorily, they are written down and placed in a folder that the student will take into group. Goals are reviewed at the beginning of each session. Group members help one another review their goals, celebrate successes, look for the instances when goals were met and when they were not, and revise and make new goals as appropriate. Again, younger students will need more direction and help with this process than older students, but even with younger students we want to take care that we do not impose our own agendas. We are teaching kids that they have the strength and the internal resources to make positive changes.

 ## ONE GROUP MEMBER'S SOLUTION-FOCUSED PROCESS

Jake was referred by his tenth-grade biology teacher because his grades had dropped from As to Ds and Fs in a short period of time. The counselor, Mrs. Sloan, met with Jake to explore with him this big change in his school performance. When Jake walked in and sat down, he kept his head down and did not look at her. Mrs. Sloan moved her chair from behind the desk, closer to him. She opened the conversation by asking Jake to tell her why he thought the biology teacher had referred him. Jake kept his head down as he reported that his grades were "bad." Then Mrs. Sloan asked Jake to tell her what he believed was the reason for his grades being "bad."

She kept her tone interested because she was curious to know how Jake saw this situation.

After some gentle prompting, Jake told her that his parents had separated. He was living with his mother while his older brother (who had a lot of conflict with their mother) had left to live with their father. He said he now rarely saw his brother or his father. Jake described spending most of his time at home in his room listening to music. He had no interest in studying. He felt that biology was the only subject he really needed to study, and that was why his grades were so bad there and not as bad in other classes.

Mrs. Sloan asked Jake if he woke one day and things were better, what would be different? He responded that his family would be back together and he and his brother would be sharing a room again. The counselor had hoped that his response would have something to do with his biology grade, but, when it did not, she shifted gears.

The goals that Jake set had to do with finding ways to spend more time with his brother and less time in his room alone. Collaboratively, Jake and his counselor looked for the strengths Jake had to make the change he wanted and he took these goals with him into group.

At the first group meeting, Jake had tried to call his brother but had not received a call back. He felt discouraged. Group members picked up on the fact that he had made the call and strongly supported him. They asked what kind of relationship Jake had with his brother before the family breakup. The leader supported the group members' interest in pursuing a deeper understanding of Jake's situation as it applied to their own lives. She helped them to find exceptions in Jake's discouragement and their own—that is, situations in which they had been successful.

Over the next two meetings, with the group's support and after a few conversations with his brother, Jake changed his goal to speaking with his brother several times a week. The group encouraged him to ask for more. He also asked his mother to arrange for him to spend four weekend nights a month with his father and brother. During the 6 weeks that the group worked together, Jake gained an increased ability to see that he had power in his situation and could make things better for himself. His biology grades also improved.

Examining Jake's experience and the counselor's work with him, we can see the important elements of solution-focused goal setting. Jake defined the problem, not the counselor. His goals were stated behaviorally, specifically, and in small positive steps. Jake modified his goals and made new goals as his work in the group progressed.

Ongoing Evaluation of Progress

In Jake's story we can observe shifts in goals as changes take place. With some success and group support Jake began to expect more. Group members may discover that they have bitten off too much and have to set more realistic goals in order to experience success. Our tasks as leaders are to help each member succeed, finding when plans have worked and modifying plans as necessary. At the end of a six-session group some members will have met their initial goals and others will need more time.

As we evaluate, we consider individual and group progress. In SOS groups we do not wait until the last group meeting to evaluate the members' experience of the group. We actively ask for ongoing feedback regarding how the group is working for the members.

The Psychoeducational Counseling Approach

From a psychoeducational aspect, we are making use of the SOS group setting to educate members about psychological concepts that they can use to help meet their goals. Leading SOS groups means we again have teaching roles. Our intention is teach group members to use thinking to manage feelings and actions. Table 2.2 illustrates how SOS didactic material and activities are correlated with the American School Counselor Association (ASCA) National Standards (Campbell & Dahir, 1997) to educate students in six skill-development content areas:

TABLE 2.2

Correlation of ASCA Personal/Social Development Standards with SOS Group Topics

ASCA Personal/Social Development Standards	SOS Primary Group Topics	SOS Intermediate Group Topics	SOS Secondary Group Topics
A. Students will acquire the knowledge, attitudes and interpersonal skills to help them understand and respect themselves and others.	SKA-P-1 SKA-P-2 SKA-P-3 ICS-P-1 ICS-P-2 ICS-P-3	SKA-I-1 SKA-I-2 SKA-I-3 ICS-I-1 ICS-I-2 ICS-I-3	SKA-S-1 SKA-S-2 SKA-S-3 ICS-S-1 ICS-S-2 ICS-S-3
B. Students will make decisions, set goals and take necessary action to achieve goals.	DM-P-1 DM-P-2 DM-P-3 CR-P-1 CR-P-2 CR-P-3	DM-I-1 DM-I-2 DM-I-3 CR-I-1 CR-I-2 CR-I-3	DM-S-1 DM-S-2 DM-S-3 CR-S-1 CR-S-2 CR-S-3
C. Students will understand safety and survival skills.	SC-P-1 SC-P-2 SC-P-3 RB-P-1 RB-P-2 RB-P-3	SC-I-1 SC-I-2 SC-I-3 RB-I-1 RB-I-2 RB-I-3	SC-S-1 SC-S-2 SC-S-3 RB-S-1 RB-S-2 RB-S-3

self-knowledge and acceptance; interpersonal and communication skills, including appreciation of diversity; responsible behavior and personal responsibility; conflict resolution; decision making and problem solving; and self-care and self-management.

As leaders of an SOS group we are always listening for the way in which didactic material relates to the individual group member's goals. For example, the leader of the group that included Don and Barry used didactic material to help Don with his difficulties with impulsivity. The leader used the I–Statement activity in an attempt to help Don and others with the goal of slowing down responses and improving communication. The leader, making use of the group process, turned to the other members for help. The help she asked for is an essential part of the solution-focused process; she asks for an exception to Don's sense of failure with the activity. The leader took the opportunity to teach and reinforce with the whole group how to solve problems using the solution-focused process. She did this through enlisting the help of the group and using the didactic material.

Making use of the psychoeducational component of the SOS model requires us to be well prepared for group meetings. We take each of the content areas and plan activities to teach the concepts. The following guidelines, adapted from Brown (2004), are helpful in planning activities:

- Be clear about what you want to accomplish and communicate that to group members.
- Consider the maturity level of the group in terms of the depth of the didactic material and the length of time dedicated to it.
- Make connections between members' individual goals and the activity. Involve members in this conversation to assess and develop their comprehension.
- Choose activities that require active participation from members.
- Create opportunities to practice new skills.

Skill Development Content

The SOS group model can be set up as one or more six-session units. You might think of it as a group six-pack! The leader has the flexibility to choose whether to make groups available to a large number of students with each receiving one six-session unit or to provide for groups of longer duration for fewer numbers of students, with each member participating in two or more six-session units in succession.

Each unit includes a session from each of the following topic areas:

1. **Self-Knowledge and Acceptance.** Students will learn about their abilities, interests, and personal characteristics. When students learn to identify their strengths and the areas in which they need to improve, their sense of self is strengthened.
2. **Interpersonal and Communication Skills.** Students will develop positive interpersonal relationships and communication skills to promote positive interactions with one another. Students will also learn to value differences and uniqueness among people.
3. **Responsible Behavior and Personal Responsibility.** Students will develop personal responsibility for their behavior. They will

learn how attitudes and perceptions can affect behavior, how feelings and behaviors are related to goals and consequences, and how behavior can be changed.

4. **Conflict Resolution.** Students will learn nonviolent ways to resolve conflict. Students will also learn styles of cooperative behavior and healthy expressions of anger.

5. **Decision Making and Problem Solving.** Students will learn the steps for making effective decisions. They will also learn the factors that influence change and decision making. Emphasis will be placed on responsibility and individual choice.

6. **Self-Care and Self-Management.** Students will learn how to express feelings in healthy ways, advocate for themselves, manage their time, and manage stress.

Skills from these six areas are taught with each subsequent six-session unit, but at a level of increased sophistication and depth. This spiraling curriculum systematically builds on previous skills. See Appendixes 2.A, 2.B, and 2.C for illustrations of lesson topics for primary, intermediate, and secondary levels for single, double, and triple six-session units. Chapter 8 includes the lesson plans, activities, handouts, and reproducibles for three six-session units for primary, intermediate and secondary levels—fifty-four lesson plans in all.

Summary

- SOS groups are brief groups that integrate group, solution-focused, and psychoeducational counseling approaches.
- SOS groups, as with other group counseling models, go through predictable developmental stages.
- SOS group leaders use interaction in the group to strengthen members' senses of themselves as capable and responsible.
- SOS group leaders teach the solution-focused approach from the first interview, looking for strengths to help kids solve their own problems through collaborative goal setting.
- Psychoeducational activities are used to develop skills in six content areas: self-knowledge and acceptance; interpersonal and communication skills; responsible behavior and personal responsibility; conflict resolution; decision making and problem solving; and self-care and self-management. To make these group activities effective, thoughtful planning is required.
- The skill-development activities are used to support members in making changes that will help them meet their individual goals.

APPENDIX 2.A

Primary-Level Single- and Multiple-Unit Group Schedule

Topic Area	Unit I Sessions 1–6	Unit II Sessions 7–12	Unit III Sessions 13–18
Self-Knowledge and Acceptance	Discovery Hunt	Identify Your Feelings	Showing Your Feelings
Interpersonal and Communication Skills	Formulating I-Statements	How To Recognize a Good Listener	Name Game
Responsible Behavior	Accepting Responsibility Versus Blaming Others	Welcome to Manners Land!	Something I've Done To Improve Our World
Conflict Resolution	The Turtle Technique for Tempering Anger	Using Refusal Skills	Expressing Your Anger
Decision Making	Consequences of Choices and Decisions	Goal Wheel	Overcoming Obstacles to Goals
Self-Care	Relaxing	Affirm Your Body!	My Body and Me
	Graduation or continue to Unit II	*Graduation or continue to Unit III*	*Graduation*

APPENDIX 2.B

Intermediate-Level Single- and Multiple-Unit Group Schedule

Topic Area	Unit I Sessions 1–6	Unit II Sessions 7–12	Unit III Sessions 13–18
Self-Knowledge and Acceptance	Getting To Know You and Me	"WANTED"	How We See Ourselves: Self-Assessment, Sharing, and Discussion"
Interpersonal and Communication Skills	I–Messages: Still No Substitute!	The Active Listener	The Clique Phenomenon
Responsible Behavior	Steps for Solving a Problem Responsibly	Manners Land: Intermediate	Have to … Choose to …
Conflict Resolution	Exploring Alternatives to Conflict	Up and Down Escalators: Raising and Lowering the Level of Conflict	What Am I Thinking?
Decision Making	Decisions, Decisions!	Setting and Attaining Goals	Decisions and Outcomes
Self-Care	The Breath of Life	S–T–O–P That Thought	The Memory Poem
	Graduation or continue to Unit II	*Graduation or continue to Unit III*	*Graduation*

APPENDIX 2.C

Secondary-Level Single- and Multiple-Unit Group Schedule

Topic Area	Unit I Sessions 1–6	Unit II Sessions 7–12	Unit III Sessions 13–18
Self-Knowledge and Acceptance	Something About Me You Wouldn't Know Unless I Told You	How We See Ourselves	Who Am I?
Interpersonal and Communication Skills	The Assert Formula	Mastering Assertive Communication	Group Discussion Roles
Responsible Behavior	Improving the Study Habit	Freedom and Responsibility	Who's in Charge?
Conflict Resolution	Assessing Anger Styles	Problem Solving: The Win–Win Strategy	Managing Moods
Decision Making	Decisions, Decisions!	Approval and Consequences	Looking Back on a Decision I Made
Self-Care	Success Bombardment	Centering and Balancing	Effectively Managing Time
	Graduation or continue to Unit II	*Graduation or continue to Unit III*	*Graduation*

3

Being an SOS Group Leader

Facilitating and Trusting the Group

Healthy Group Boundaries

Leadership and Self-Awareness

Group Leadership Skills

Facilitating and Trusting the Group

Group counseling differs from individual counseling. Facilitation is built on a different set of skills and circumstances and the context of the group is used for therapeutic benefit.

No Longer the Solo Helper

Being a group leader is one of the most rewarding experiences you will ever have as a mental health professional. It is a modality with great therapeutic potential that is largely due to peer relationships and dynamics in the room. To make use of the members' power to help one another we have to let go of the familiar position of being the only helper. Making use of the group's help requires a shift in our thinking and our interventions. In SOS groups the required shift is to the facilitation of helpful communication that is solution-focused between group members. Notice the efforts by the leaders of the following two groups.

 TURNING TO THE GROUP FOR ASSISTANCE

One of the members of a high school group, John, was having a really bad day. John had fallen back into old patterns; he was feeling bad about himself.

In this situation the leader looked around the group and asked another group member what he believed John needed right then. When the member responded that he didn't know, the leader followed up with the same question to the rest of the group. Another member said that she thought John just needed a chance to be disappointed with himself before anyone tried to help him. The leader asked John if that sounded helpful to him and he said that he thought so. The leader then began a discussion about what was helpful to the members when they were feeling disappointed with themselves.

The leader of a group of first graders had the group involved in an art project when Sally stopped and crumpled up her work, saying she didn't like it. Using what she knew about Sally, the leader spoke to the entire group. She said that Sally was having a hard time with the project and needed their help. The leader asked what group members believed would help Sally start a new piece. One girl said that she would like to sit beside Sally if Sally wanted a partner on the project. Sally said that she didn't want any help, so the leader thanked the volunteer for her offer and asked for more ideas, including any that Sally might have. Sally then said that she thought a larger piece of paper would help her. The leader told Sally she was welcome to get the larger paper. Following up on the interaction, the leader invited the group to talk about times when they did not want help and times when they offered help and were turned down. She used the experience to focus on problem solving in such situations.

Respect for the Group

In each of these examples the leaders encouraged members to assist one another and, in so doing, created opportunities for members to develop a stronger sense of themselves as capable individuals. The leaders sent messages to group members that said, "I respect each of you and your ability to help one another." Leaders' interventions can be summarized in the following points:

- Make a practice of slowing your response time in order to resist too quickly coming in to "help." This gives you the opportunity to make a choice of what kind of intervention to use.
- Actively share responsibility by requesting specific assistance from individual members or the whole group.
- If an initial effort to enlist group members is unsuccessful, choose follow-up interventions that continue to demonstrate that you believe the group members can help one another.
- Stay grounded with a sense of what will be helpful and fluid enough to respond to the unexpected.
- Keep a playful spirit.
- Choose and frame requests for assistance that are within the capability of the members.
- In SOS groups, solution-focused communication is encouraged between group members.

Healthy Group Boundaries

The issue of boundaries in the counseling format becomes more complex with groups than with individual counseling. Consideration of what it means to have healthy boundaries can assist all group members in having a supportive growth experience.

Establishing Safety and Predictability

Healthy boundaries provide, in large part, the "container" for the group's work. We use the word *container* to imply an environment in which group members can feel surrounded by the experience of being safe and valued. How this environment is created will vary from leader to leader. The following suggestions are basics we encourage you to use:

- Stop and start the group on time each meeting.
- Keep meeting time and place consistent.
- Provide a meeting place that supports confidentiality.
- Give group members notice if there is a need for a change in the logistics.
- Provide a predictable format.
- Be consistent in the ways you respond to members.
- Maintain members' confidentiality.

Maintaining confidentiality in school settings is an essential, complex skill. We must be vigilant in keeping confidential what members share with us, but it is not a simple task when working with kids. A workable framework can be provided by making it clear to group members that you will not share their secrets, but that you will share with important adults in their lives how the adults can be helpful to them. There will be times, of course, when even this framework requires thoughtful exceptions.

Members rely on the group leader's consistency in responding to them and to their problems. It is important for each of us to be as clear as possible about what we believe is helpful about being in a group. It is essential that we choose, to the best of our ability, interventions that maintain that safe environment.

Establishing and Maintaining Group Agreements

The "container" for the group's work is also supported through the use of group agreements that set the ground rules for member participation. Leadership tasks include seeing that there are group agreements and maintaining them. In maintaining group agreements our job is not to become the Agreement Police. We have the responsibility to establish clear, straightforward agreements and to notice when an agreement is not respected. With younger children the leader has to take a greater degree of control to maintain sufficient order in the environment for the group to function. Often, with both older and younger kids, there is the pull to be authoritarian too quickly with regard to agreements. There are situations in which the leader must quickly enforce a boundary. On the other hand, staying calm and exploratory and using group members' input in the face of boundary violations can lead to important behavior change for group members.

Adolescents will watch to see how fairly the group is managed and the boundaries maintained, but with this age group there is more room to involve the

A MEMBER BRINGS CANDY TO GROUP

The leader of a fourth-grade group noticed that one of the members, David, was eating candy. This group had an agreement not to bring food to group unless there was enough to share with everyone. This rule had not been broken before, and David was normally overly compliant. The leader decided to ask David if he had forgotten the agreement or if he had brought the candy to share. When David said he had forgotten and did not want to share, the leader looked to the group for their feelings and what they thought would be the best way to solve the problem. Several group members thought that it was a "dumb rule" and that David should eat his candy. The leader acknowledged the members' feelings and said that they could revisit the rule another day, but it still stood today. She turned to David and asked him how he wanted to solve the problem he had today and they worked out a solution.

 A MISSING MEMBER

In a high school group, Alice stopped showing up for sessions. When the leader checked with the classroom teacher, she found that Alice was leaving class to attend the group. The agreement was that members would attend each group unless they were ill. Alice was not ill; she was spending group time talking with friends. Once the leader found out what was happening, she requested that Alice come to the next group meeting to decide if she wanted to continue with the group. Alice came to the meeting and said that she *did* want to remain in the group, but the next week she did not show up and was not ill. The leader talked about the problem with group members and found that they were feeling "dissed" by Alice. The leader was unclear about how much room to give Alice. Group members were able to verbalize that Alice's inconsistency interfered with how safe they felt in the group. The leader used the input to decide that it was in the best interest of the group for Alice to no longer be a member.

These two examples demonstrate dilemmas regarding agreements. It may appear that it would be easier for both leaders to ignore the boundary violations or just to step in to stop the behavior in question. It is our opinion, however, that real value is in the use of group agreements to teach problem solving, the importance of sticking with agreements, and how behavior affects others. Finding the delicate balance between involving group members in decision making while clearly holding final decision-making power is an essential goal of group leadership.

 Details for creating group agreements are discussed in Chapter 5 and examples of group agreements are in the forms section in Appendix 4.A.

> ## Tips for Maintaining Group Agreements
>
> - Keep the number of agreements to a workable minimum.
> - Make sure that agreements take into account the developmental level(s) of the members.
> - Make agreements that are easy to understand and are unambiguous.
> - Resist taking on the role of the "Agreement Police."
> - Stay aware of agreements and bring violations to the group's attention, so that a remedy can be found in a timely way.
> - Younger kids will require more direction to maintain agreements.
> - Post group agreements as a helpful reminder.
> - Use the maintenance of boundaries stated in group agreements as a tool for teaching problem solving, especially with older kids.

Leadership and Self-Awareness

This section provides three exercises regarding your expectations, prejudices, and vulnerabilities. Taking the time to write out your responses will make these exercises more useful to you. Writing your responses will also initiate a practice of reflecting on your personal experience as a group leader that will be extremely valuable to you.

Knowing Your Expectations

What are your expectations for how members of your group should respond? Do you expect them to be polite or rude? Do you expect them to let you know how happy they are to be in the group, or do you expect them to be resistant? Do you expect them to make great progress or no progress? Our expectations will affect the whole group as well as individual members because our expectations have a strong impact on what gets our attention, and what gets our attention normally flourishes. Clarifying expectations and being aware of expectations make it possible to better choose what flourishes in our groups.

A common problem for new group leaders is expecting greater maturity from the group members than is possible. If we are aware of our expectations and aware that we might be wrong, we can be open to discovering the group members' current functional levels. We can then help them move forward, rather than being frustrated about their lack of maturity. We invite you to examine your expectations by working through the following exercise.

Exercise

> *A sixth-grade group is meeting for the first time. There are six members: three boys and three girls. Three have been referred for help due to a significant loss in their lives—two from divorce and one from a family tragedy. Of the other three, one has been referred because of impulse problems, another for friendship difficulties, and another for academic problems. Stop and take a few minutes to write down any expectations you might have with regard to being the leader of this group. Then consider how these expectations might affect the group and its individual members. Would gender affect your expectations, and if so, how?*

Knowing Your Prejudices

Prejudice can be defined as a preconceived opinion or judgment. The strongest position we can take is being aware of what our prejudices are rather than wishing we did not have them. As group leaders we are exposed. Our group members are watching us and will notice how we respond to each member and to the whole group. A simple example of prejudice might be the belief that "middle school kids always push limits." Acting from this prejudicial notion, a group leader might manage the group too strongly in regard to agreements. Some members may need this kind of direction, but others—who need opportunities to be more assertive—may be inhibited. When we acknowledge our prejudices to ourselves, we are in better positions to make choices about our responses. It will be possible to stay curious about each group and group member and to lead much more effective groups. In the following exercise, we ask you to examine your prejudices.

Exercise

> *An adolescent group has just added a new member. There are now four White members, two Hispanic members, one Black member, and one Asian member. The new member is a White male with a tattoo on his forearm. What thoughts come to mind about how this new member will affect the group? Stop and take a few minutes to honestly and privately list your prejudices regarding the members as described. How would gender affect your feelings toward any one of these members? Remember—our prejudices can be either negative or positive. Judging yourself is not allowed in this exercise. The insight you gain will be useful in making choices as you work with groups.*

Knowing Your Vulnerabilities

Again, while we are watching the group, the group is watching us. Group members will notice what makes us smile and what we respond to, in negative or positive ways. Being a group leader will show us our vulnerabilities perhaps more quickly than any other type of mental health work. The most productive stance is to stay aware of what we know upsets us and to stay open to learning something new about ourselves. For example, a common problem is that members may not like the group and do not want to come. Do you know how you usually respond to not feeling liked or being told that what you have to offer is not valuable? You can be certain that at times you will encounter such situations. Being as aware as possible of our vulnerabilities helps us respond rather than react impulsively in situations in which our "buttons" get pushed.

We are not suggesting that a group leader should never express negative feelings; rather, we are suggesting that greater self-awareness will give us more flexibility. With more choices there is the greater possibility of an effective response. In the exercise below, we ask you to consider what your vulnerabilities would be in this group leadership situation.

Exercise

> *A fourth-grade group has been meeting for 3 weeks. One of the members, Kelly, had been an active participant in the group at the beginning but had clearly shifted into a negative stance toward both the leader and a particularly shy member, Lorie. During an activity, Kelly called Lorie "dumb." When the leader turned to speak to Kelly, Kelly glared at the leader and said, "I don't like you or this group. It doesn't help me, or anybody else." Put yourself in the leader's place. What feelings do you have at this moment? Stop and take a few minutes to privately list what those feelings are.*

The practice of keeping a private record of our personal reactions to our groups can go a long way toward our becoming more self-aware and effective as group leaders. We can often be our own best supervisors as we notice patterns in our responses that could be more effective, and we experience the relief that comes with putting our thoughts and feelings into words on paper.

Group Leadership Skills

Creating a predictable, safe group environment that grows in self-awareness and has specific group skills is the foundation of effective group leadership. Skills are the "know how" of group work. Most of the skills we list generalize to any group, but some are specific to running SOS groups. For each skill listed below, there is a definition and an example with brief commentary.

Empathic Listening

Empathic listening is both listening for content and seeking to understand the feelings and experience behind the content. This skill is often referred to as active listening (Brown, 2004).

 ### NO CHANCE TO PLAY

Sam, a third-grade group member, told the group about his disappointment that his parents were not letting him play after school because they had met with his teacher about his bad grades. The group leader watched Sam's face, looking for what he felt about what he said. She noticed she experienced a sad feeling herself.

Points to keep in mind:

- In empathic listening we are asked to actively put ourselves in the place of group members, seeking to understand the experience from their perception. Our own physical and emotional responses can be our best sources of information.
- We let the group know that we are listening via our nonverbal responses, such as keeping good eye contact and leaning toward the speaker slightly. In SOS groups we are modeling listening and directly teaching group members how to be helpful to one another by listening to understand.
- Notice where your own empathy went in the example. Did it go to Sam, his parents, or his teacher? While there may be many reasons to empathize with the adults, empathically listening to Sam will help us as group leaders to understand his disappointment and to respond effectively.

Empathic Responding

Empathic responding can be either verbal or nonverbal. It requires us to include both the content and the interpretation of what we have heard (Brown, 2004).

 ### RESPONDING EMPATHICALLY

[Returning to the example:] The leader sympathetically nodded to Sam and then turned to another member who was also being restricted at home for grade problems. The leader said, "Corey, you and Sam are both having to stay inside after you get home to do schoolwork. Can you think of something that might help Sam?" Later in the group the leader had an opportunity to return to Sam and ask him if there was something more the group could do to help him today.

Points to keep in mind:

- A verbal empathic response might be to simply validate the feelings being expressed. A nonverbal empathic response might be good eye contact and a facial expression that shows concern.
- There is often so much going on simultaneously in a group that we have to choose where to direct a response.
- Sometimes it is unclear how to respond; at times, our own vulnerabilities are triggered. Giving ourselves the opportunity to reflect is essential.
- It is helpful to develop the skill to attend in a way that makes it possible to return to something that happened or was said earlier. This conveys the importance of members' concerns.

Use of Questions

In the SOS model we focus on what is working instead of what is not working for members. We use questions to get new information to create and improve on members' solutions (Murphy, 1997). A goal for the group leader is to teach members to ask themselves and one another solution-focused questions.

 Chapter 5 provides more details on asking solution-focused questions.

 USING QUESTIONS TO CHANGE A PLAN

Lauren, a member of a high school group, had been working on controlling her anger but had an explosive episode with her mother the night before the group met. The leader listened carefully to Lauren and empathized with how ashamed she felt to have acted out with her mother. Then the leader asked Lauren to describe for the group exactly when she believed things had started to go wrong for her in the exchange with her mother. After Lauren had finished her description, the leader turned to the group and asked what questions members had so that they could help Lauren come up with a revision of her plan for controlling her anger.

Points to keep in mind:

- Use of questions to get a deeper understanding of what is being said is an invaluable skill. It is easy to overuse questions, however, when we have an agenda. Avoid asking a question that is really a statement, or when there is only one correct answer from our point of view.

- Use questions to explore; make questions open ended, avoiding questions that lead to "yes" or "no" answers. Questions that invite responses from all members are helpful and can encourage member interaction.

Reviewing

In reviewing we provide summary or reflection of what we have heard from one member or a number of members (Brown, 2004). In order to review, we must have been paying attention so that we can remember what has been said.

 REVIEWING PROVES USEFUL

In a seventh-grade group, a number of members began the session describing the ways in which they had not been successful with their goals. The leader listened carefully and was able to reflect and summarize for the group. One of the members then said that, in fact, she had made a little progress and explained what it had been. The leader acknowledged this added information and asked the member what input she might have for those who had not felt successful at all.

Points to keep in mind:

- It is usually not the exact words that we want but, rather, the essence as we understood it.
- With reviewing we can discover that we have misunderstood or that there was more to be heard.
- Reviewing gives members the opportunity to listen to the leader's perception of what has been said.

Confronting

Confrontation is asking a member or the group to look at behavior and its impact and consequences. To be helpful, the confrontation cannot be aggressive and cannot be an attempt to sway others to our point of view (Ormont, 1992; Rutan & Stone, 2001).

 CONFRONTATION TO MAINTAIN A BOUNDARY

The leader of a kindergarten group faced a difficult situation with a group of four that had been meeting for ten weeks. Two of the members, who had been referred for behavior control problems, were resistant to following agreements. These agreements included not turning off the only light in the windowless meeting room. The leader had attempted to work with them in a number of different ways to maintain this boundary. After spending time thinking about the situation and consulting with a colleague, she decided to confront the two with the fact that the group could not meet without light in the room. She invited the group, including the two light switch culprits, to come up with a solution. With the leader's help, the group decided to start each session by covering the switch. This confrontation was successful because the decision was not aggressive and was based on relationships that had been established in the group.

Points to keep in mind:

- Confronting is a leadership skill that must be used judiciously. Brown (2004) suggested that before using confrontation we honestly ask ourselves if the confrontation will be helpful to both the member *and* the group. Brown further recommended that if we do not feel completely confident that confrontation will be helpful, we should avoid the use of this strategy.
- Successful confrontation requires empathy. When you are feeling strong emotions of your own, it is not time to confront. Wait until you have given yourself time to think and sort out your emotions.
- Confronting before a sense of safety and a therapeutic relationship have been established is not likely to be helpful.
- In the solution-focused approach there are four ideas that are confronted and challenged. These ideas are blaming others, seeing change as impossible, invalidating our own or others' thoughts or feelings, and denying accountability. These four ideas will be discussed in Chapter 5.

Support

Support is the effort to create an environment where there is a sense of safety and emotional "space," and in which we communicate understanding in our responses (Rutan & Stone, 2001).

 ## USING POSITIVE MIRRORING TO SUPPORT

The leader of a fifth-grade group noticed that Daniel, who had difficulty speaking in the group, was always on time. At the beginning of a session, the leader turned to Daniel and, leaning slightly forward in her chair, smiled and said, "Daniel, you really help this group get started each week by being on time and ready to work. I appreciate you, Daniel."

Remember:

- This simple intervention demonstrates the use of support. The leader used both verbal and nonverbal responses, positively mirrored the member, and highlighted a group value that she wanted to encourage.

- Support is an important skill for SOS group leaders. Be on the lookout for what you want to encourage and for who needs encouragement.

- Being supportive is a skill that we want to model and develop in group members. Often, the best way to support is to pay attention through nonverbal communication, such as eye contact, smiles, and a body posture that includes uncrossed arms and a slight leaning toward group members.

- Verbal communication to support includes active listening and empathic responses. *Positive mirroring* is another verbal support used to promote healthy growth in group members' senses of self. With this skill we reflect the abilities, impacts, and unique qualities of the group as a whole or of an individual in a way that clearly says, "I value this about you."

Connecting and Disconnecting the Dots

Connecting and disconnecting the dots is an intervention based on having paid attention to the simultaneous actions, comments, concerns, and interactions in the group meeting. Using what we have noticed we speak to the group about specific similarities or differences.

CONNECTING TWO DOTS

In a high school group, Charlie told the story of losing a book that one of his teachers had loaned him to work on an assignment. He was feeling disappointed in himself and was at a loss as to what to do. Earlier in the group another member, James, had talked about confronting a problem in a new way that included telling a friend the truth even though it was hard. The leader turned from Charlie to James and said, "I'm thinking that you have talked about something today that could help Charlie." Turning back to Charlie she asked, "Do you know what I'm talking about?"

DISCONNECTING DOTS

At the end of a meeting, the leader of a sixth-grade group noticed that two of the members who usually did not actively participate had been more active. She turned to each of them and then to the group and said, "This group felt different to me today. Has it felt different to any of you?" No one responded, so she continued, "Well, I really appreciated hearing how Tommy and Ellen are working on their goals. We all have so much to teach one another."

In the preceding scenarios, it is important to notice that:

- In the high school example, the leader made the connection between the two situations and then encouraged the members to make use of the connection.
- The leader in the middle school example not only pointed out a difference but also supported the two members and encouraged a group value.
- We are promoting individual relationships, group cohesiveness, and deepening understanding within the group when we connect and disconnect the dots.
- This strategy is best not overused, so that its impact is not diluted. At first it might be helpful to ration yourself to one dot-connect and one dot-disconnect per group session.

Use of Group Interaction

Group interaction calls on many of the skills discussed above, such as questioning, reviewing, and connecting and disconnecting the dots. The express purpose is to encourage members to interact with one another more effectively and further the goals of the group (Yalom & Leszcz, 2005).

 AN UNPREDICTED RESPONSE

In a five-member first-grade group, the leader pointed out that two members, Sarah and Janie, had both used the same colors in their art projects. The leader asked Janie to look at Sarah's work and notice the colors. With a frown Janie looked over at what Sarah had worked on and started to respond negatively toward Sarah. The leader quickly interrupted and said, "I especially like the way each of you has done your work today."

- When we encourage interaction, we let go of that "solo helper" position. We send the message that members are in group to help themselves and that they can also be helpful to one another.
- In the example above the leader had predicted a different response in her effort to encourage interaction. When the response was negative, she moved to interrupt and block the potentially shaming feedback. The leader came back with a response that worked to protect both members from shame. Our efforts will not always go the way we hope.
- As group leaders we can encourage group interaction by providing opportunities for giving and receiving constructive and respectful feedback among members. The key words here are "respectful" and "constructive." It is our responsibility to protect members from being shamed in the group while we encourage interaction.

A HELPFUL RESPONSE

A third-grade group had been meeting for three weeks. Two members, Leon and Zack, were especially verbal and physically active. In the middle of a session Leon jumped up and left his seat, going to the back of the room. The leader turned to Zack and asked him what he thought Leon needed to help him come back into the circle. Zack looked at Leon and said, "I think he needs me to tell him that I need his help." The leader nodded and Zack said, "Leon, come help me." In a few minutes Leon returned to the circle and sat down.

In this vignette:

- The intervention worked out more the way it was intended.

- The leader used a technique called *bridging* (Ormont, 1992), which can be particularly effective in encouraging member interaction. Just as the word implies, the technique is designed to build and strengthen connections between group members. We might, for example, ask one member what he or she would choose as a next step with the problem another group member is having. Choosing which member to bridge with another requires considering similarities and differences.

Collaboratively Establishing Goals and Finding Solutions

This leadership skill requires us to know the solution-focused process and to turn to group members for their input and expertise. Being collaborative means that we give up the idea that we know best. We make use of the members' and the group's strengths.

HELP THROUGH COLLABORATION

A high school group had been meeting for five weeks. Kendra's best friend had been killed in a car wreck and Kendra had joined the group to help her grieve this terrible loss. At the beginning of the meeting Kendra told the group that she had made no progress on her goal of creating a scrapbook to honor the lost friendship. Another group member, Doug, who was always protective of Kendra, said to her that maybe it was too soon to try this. The leader acknowledged Doug's concern for Kendra and then asked what ideas the group had about what Kendra might do that would be helpful to her. Mattie turned to Kendra and said that looking at old photos every day and remembering good times had helped her with her own loss. She asked Kendra how that sounded. Kendra said she thought she could make that her goal for the next week.

Notice how:

- SOS group leaders make use of the group and its individual members to help kids learn to find solutions to their own difficulties through goal setting.
- SOS group leaders maintain a group environment that helps members with their goals.
- The maturity level of the group members is taken into account as we teach and support the solution-focused process.
- The SOS group leader monitors group member progress, so that as goals are met or modified, new goals can be established with input from the leader and other group members.

Tips for Group Leaders

- Learn to count to ten for the times when you need to buy some time to decide how to respond.
- Practice saying "I made a mistake," and use the phrase when the situation arises.
- Learning to deal with the threat of being abandoned is helpful.
- Schedule a break for yourself before and after leading a group. This practice provides you with time to organize materials and the room before group, and time to complete group notes and evaluate after the group ends.
- Journaling is an excellent tool to recommend and to use for yourself.
- Careful listening is a gift.
- Being aware of the developmental level of group members is essential. Expecting more maturity than is available will lead to frustration for the leader and the group.
- Know your expectations, prejudices, and vulnerabilities.
- Members are watching you; this provides you with the opportunity to model what you want to teach.
- Whatever we give our attention to will flourish in our groups.
- Maintain your sense of humor and playful spirit.

Summary

- In becoming a group leader we must give up the idea that we are the "solo helper" in the room and facilitate group members' helping one another.

- Successful group work requires creating a safe "container" for members that includes predictability, confidentiality, understanding, and consensus on group agreements.

- Group agreements make boundaries explicit. The healthy maintenance of agreements is an essential leadership task.

- Knowing our expectations, prejudices, and vulnerabilities facilitates our development and effectiveness as group leaders.

- Group leadership requires us to develop a set of skills that improves our ability to listen, respond, ask questions, support, and encourage group interaction.

- SOS group leadership requires us to learn the solution-focused approach so that we can teach group members how to define their problems and set goals for themselves using that process.

4 Setting Up SOS Groups in Schools

Collaborative Relationships

When counselors and others working for kids' growth in schools collaborate, their energies are particulary effective. Taking time to develop collaborative relationships is important for good group counseling outcomes.

Educating Colleagues and Parents About SOS Group Work

With SOS groups, students and counselors can work effectively and efficiently to resolve school problems in a positive manner. A good supply of student referrals requires a well-informed referral base. Cultivating your referral base of colleagues and parents requires groundwork. Take some time and educate the teachers, administrators, and parents in your school about all of the benefits of using the SOS group model. Their experience may have been that groups are problem focused and organized to deal only with specific topics such as grief or anger management. They may also perceive that groups are unstructured situations in which students engage in unproductive griping. When teachers, administrators, and parents understand the SOS group model they will make appropriate referrals and come to appreciate the skills students learn as they make progress toward their goals.

There are numerous ways to educate colleagues and parents about the SOS group program. Announcements at meetings for faculty and the PTA, newsletters, flyers, information brochures, program overviews, and Web sites can be used to inform teachers, administrators, and parents about available groups. The following are selling points to use when you talk about SOS groups:

- Counselors are able to help a larger number of students in the school. They have the opportunities to work with students in settings that are like real life, which leads to counselor consultation that is relevant and real. SOS groups are effective with a wide variety of problems or diagnoses.

- Students experience an environment where there are lots of helpers—their counselor and their fellow group members. They experience support for making positive changes.
- Students have the opportunity to talk about their problem situations, and they quickly learn to use the solution-focused process to address those problems. Students learn how to find the exceptions to the problem and develop a plan for themselves to resolve their problems.
- Each student can work on very different individual goals while working as a group to help everyone follow the solution-focused process. Goals are the students' goals, and not those of the counselor, parents, teachers, or principal.
- Group members learn real skills for self-awareness, personal responsibility, interpersonal communication, decision making, and conflict resolution.
- Students graduate from SOS groups with an improved ability to master problems and act on their own behalf in a constructive manner.

 See Appendix 4.A for sample teacher and parent group information handouts and sample needs assessment forms for elementary, middle, and high-school groups.

Using a Needs Assessment

Involving your staff and parents in a needs assessment is a quick and effective way to communicate about groups. A needs assessment gives valuable information about students' needs from the perspectives of teachers, administrators, parents, and students themselves. Needs data gives counselors additional support to use counseling time and resources for group interventions (Loesch & Ritchie, 2005). The needs assessment is an excellent accountability tool because it provides baseline data about members that can be used for comparison to data at the end of groups to show growth. Decide from whom needs assessment information is to be obtained—teachers alone or a wider audience of parents, students, and administrators. The needs assessment is an excellent way to illustrate the purpose of groups and gain recommendations for group members, times to meet, and specific skills to incorporate (Greenburg, 2003).

Tips for Needs Assessment

- Give teachers and administrators adequate time at the beginning of the school year to get to know their students and have an idea who should be priorities for group participation (Metcalf, 2002).
- Allow each teacher to designate their first, second, and third choices of students for participation in groups (Greenberg, 2003). The counselor will make

the selections to form each group, but it will be helpful to know the teacher's priorities.

- Ask about the teacher's reasons for recommending the students for group.

- Be sure to obtain a needs assessment form from every teacher. If the teacher has no students to refer at a given time, have the teacher note that and sign and return the form.

- Give teachers, administrators, and parents an example of the kind of response expected on the form.

Turning Referrals Into Goal Negotiations

One of our best tools for developing a collaborative environment is goal-focused conversations with our referral sources. Berg and Steiner (2003) discuss the typical referral situation. Most adults—such as teachers and parents—who refer a child for group counseling have a fairly good idea of the problem. They might even have some good ideas of what is needed to remedy the problem. Yet, when asked to explain the kinds of behaviors they would like to see, they have difficulty being specific. Frequently they return to asking "why" the kid is behaving that way or repeating what the kid is doing wrong. Therefore, it is often the counselor's job to translate the problem statement into potential solutions or goals. This is achieved by asking the adults to describe what they would consider signs of a successful outcome in concrete, behavioral, and measurable ways. When the referring source is given the opportunity to clearly define concerns and goals, a sense of teamwork is developed and information to improve interventions is provided. In order to be helpful, the negotiated goals with the referral source should be

- described as the presence of a solution, not the absence of problems;
- described as a beginning of a solution, not an end of the problem;
- concrete, measurable, countable, specific, and behavioral;
- realistic and doable for the student involved;
- described in terms of changes in pattern of interaction;
- perceived as requiring considerable effort to achieve; and
- important to the kid as well as the adults.

Review the following dialogue to see how the counselor helped negotiate goals based on the parent's complaint.

Melody's Temper
P: *Melody has this terrible temper problem. She's even starting to hit, shove, and bite other kids.*

C: *I can see that you have very good reasons to be concerned about Melody. What would you like to see her do instead of shoving, hitting, kicking, biting, and losing her temper?*

P: *Maybe it's genetic. Her father was like that ... really hot-tempered.*

C: *I wonder what you need to see Melody doing that will tell you her temper problem is getting a little bit better?*

P: *I want her to take "no" for an answer and be nice to other kids.*

C: *It sounds like you would like to see her play well with other children, have more friends, and follow rules.*

P: *That's it. She needs to learn that there are rules every-where, that she has to learn to get along with other kids and grown-ups, and that she has to listen to people.*

C: *Those sound like reasonable things to ask of a 6-year-old. What exactly will you see her do that will tell you she's learning to play with other kids, accept "no" for an answer, and listen to grown-ups?*

P: *I will see her trying to take turns with other kids. I will see her listening to me and her teacher most of the time.*

In this dialogue the counselor helps the parent see Melody as inexperienced in the world. Metcalf (1997) recommended this as a useful strategy in working with individuals who are making a referral. In our goal negotiations we can confidently describe SOS groups as skill-building sessions that can increase kids' understanding of ways to cope in the world.

 We recommend the use of the referral forms in Appendix 4.A that allow the referring person to note the problem area and to indicate the skills that would be goals for achievement in the group.

Obtaining Parent Consent

Many school districts require parent permission for the student to participate in group counseling. Dennison (1997) recommended obtaining a parent's verbal *and* written permission to have the child included in a particular group. The process for obtaining parent consent can cause delays in getting groups started. Enlist the aid of teachers to help in the process. Since the counselor has usually not had the opportunity to get to know the students well, teachers can help by communicating with parents about the reason for recommending group counseling. The counselor can address group topics and curricula. An information brochure describing SOS groups that goes along with the parental consent request can be time-saving and valuable information for the parents. Sharon Wharton, a counselor who leads twenty-five groups per week, has another technique for obtaining parent permission (personal communication, September 21, 2005). After the initial interview she mails to the student's home an information sheet that describes the group, a parent consent form with a small signed note on colored paper attached, and a return envelope. The note says,

"Hi. Today, I talked with _____ about joining a support group. The attached letter explains how the group will be conducted. Your child expressed an interest in becoming a member. At your convenience, please discuss our conversation with your child. Thank you."

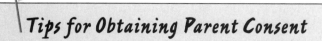

> ## Tips for Obtaining Parent Consent
>
> - Supply the referring teachers with a letter explaining group objectives to send home to parents.
> - Direct parents' questions about the reason for referral to the teacher, and questions about what will happen in group to the counselor.
> - Prepare teachers with some suggested language for reasons for referral to group.
> - Be prepared to describe SOS groups, the solution-focused process, and the competencies that will be addressed in group.

 See Appendix 4.A for sample forms for obtaining parent consent.

Naming the Group

There are endless options for naming the groups you lead with your students. For the purposes of this book, we are using the letters SOS to stand for "Strengthening Sense of Self" because this is the orientation that we take to group leadership. We like that "SOS" works for kids and teachers as a quick way to refer to groups without unnecessarily disclosing information about the students' reasons for being in group. Any name that helps to promote the idea of positive growth and strength building toward the resolution of goals will work well. Sometimes students like to name their group. We recommend keeping the name positive and avoiding names that connote a particular presenting issue, like divorce, abuse, or grief.

Working Out the Logistics

Taking the time to be responsive to all constituents in the school in working out the logistics for group will be time well spent. Doing this kind of "public relations" work will increase the perception of groups as a productive and efficient counseling intervention with benefits for improving students' academic achievement and personal and social adjustment. When group leaders can acknowledge teacher and administrator concerns and accommodate their goals, the result is a supportive environment for running groups.

Scheduling

Scheduling refers to the many options related to time, frequency, and initiation decisions for setting up groups. As you schedule, consider student availability, efficiency, teachers' demands for instructional time, and your availability. Ideally, group leaders establish groups at a regularly scheduled time when students are most likely to participate, cause the least disruption to the instructional process, and fit efficiently into the other counseling program activities. Typical group scheduling options include the following:

- Before school

- After school

- During lunch

- A regularly scheduled time each week

- An alternating time each week

- During homeroom or advisory periods

Group leaders usually plan to begin groups after a short transition period at the beginning of the school year. This allows time for teachers and administrators to get to know students and for the group leader to receive referrals of students who can benefit from group counseling. Some experienced group leaders gather needs assessment information for groups in the late spring of the previous year so that they are ready to solicit referrals and offer groups in a timely manner when school begins. The groundwork you have done with your colleagues regarding group work will pay off when you negotiate scheduling.

Choice of Room

Often the options for the locations for group work are limited. Privacy and adequate space are the most important concerns in selection of a room. Groups enjoy having some influence on the appearance of the room. The room should be a comfortable space with few distractions. Rooms that are used for multiple purposes and identified with specific activities can be problematic and are better avoided for use as group rooms. Decreasing the external stimulation in the room is also helpful. For example, toys used in play therapy can be too enticing for primary group members.

Attendance

Strategies for documenting group attendance need to be very clear and consistent. It is recommended that attendance be taken at each session using a group roster. (See Appendix 4.A for sample group rosters.) The attendance procedures at the school will influence group attendance procedures. School attendance personnel appreciate our support in providing accurate attendance information about group members.

Tips for Attendance

- *Primary-grade groups*—The group leader may pick up the students from their classroom(s) and walk with them to the group location.

- *Intermediate-grade groups*—Teachers can be given a written or e-mail reminder of the names of group members and the designated time to send the students to the group room.

- *Middle school and high school groups*

  —On the day before the group is scheduled to meet, the group leader may send reminder notes or e-mail messages to the teachers of the classes the students will miss the following day. On the day of the group meeting, the group leader may send a counselor request form to be delivered at the end of the class period just prior to the group meeting time.

  —Designate a Groups Information Board in the counseling office. On the morning of the day the group is scheduled to meet, insert counselor request forms into envelopes labeled with the group's name and meeting time and attach the envelopes to the group board. The students can come by the counseling office any time before group meeting time to pick up their counselor request form.

  —Other options include sending counselor request forms to students the day before the group meets or during first period on the day group meets, or providing a packet of counselor request forms with the student's name in advance for the duration of the group meetings. See Appendix 4.A for sample group counselor request forms.

In some schools, announcements are made over the public address system about the groups that are meeting that day. Remember to use numbers or group names that will not stigmatize group members.

Supporting Positive Behavior in Groups

Maintaining group agreements helps kids feel safe and comfortable in group settings, which sets the stage for kids to be able to address their goals and learn new skills. Many elementary and some middle school group leaders use a point system in which students earn points for adhering to agreements. Students earn points at each session and then redeem them at the end of the group for small prizes or privileges.

⊶⟶ **See Appendix 4.A for a sample elementary point sheet.**

Membership of the Group

Unlike problem-oriented groups, group members in SOS groups can each work on a different goal. Free from the need to select members with similar issues, the group leader can enroll a group of students who have a mix of personalities, inter-action styles, and goals. In Chapter 5 we address screening individual students. Here we look at the more general issues of group membership in schools.

Membership of the Group Matters

When selecting group members, consider these guidelines:

- *The student's crisis level.* Students who are actively in crisis benefit most from individual counseling. When students are really in crisis, they are in the moment so intensely that they may not be able to share with other group members. Help these students by working with them individually until they are ready for group work.
- *Vulnerability of the student to disclosures that could be detrimental.* Some students are not ready to talk about their personal issues in a group without disclosing information that could cause them embarrassment or ridicule by other students. Consider seeing individually those students whose inhibitions or boundaries about what to say are not clear.
- *Willingness to work in a group setting.* Some students prefer to work on their goals privately and are not ready to work on them with other students. Kids in this group might include those who lack a sense of what has been described as "social hunger"—a need to be accepted by peers and attain status in groups. They tend to monopolize groups without considering the needs of other kids (Swanson, 1996).
- *Ability to take turns.* The dynamics of the group setting require that members take turns talking and allow others to re-ceive the attention of the group. Lots of students need some mod-eling of this behavior and occasional reminders from the group, but consider working individually with students who seem to have a great deal of difficulty sharing attention before including them in a group.
- *Ability to relate to others positively.* It is critical that group settings be perceived as comfortable and safe for all group members

while they work on their goals for improvement. Group members will learn to discover and build upon their strengths and to encourage the same in the rest of the group. A student who has difficulty doing this can negatively influence the group. Students who demonstrate antisocial behavior, or in general show little conscience, can be harmful to other group members. Including them in a group can simply give them targets for their misbehavior. It is recommended that you work with these students individually and include them only when they show the ability to relate to others positively and not to be exploitive. When you believe that these students can be maintained in a group, they will benefit from positive peer pressure and the modeling effects that a "well-orchestrated" group offers (Swanson, 1996).

   • *Level and type of disability.* Students who have disabilities can do well in the group setting. When screening, consider carefully whether their disabilities will make them unable to participate fully or set them up to be disliked. When you include students with disabilities, construct groups that can encourage the students' full participation by modifying the material if necessary, selecting compatible group members, and arranging accommodations that support and include the students.

   • *Single-gender or mixed-gender groups.* Consider the student's developmental age and in which type of group the student would be the most comfortable. Weigh the effect of gender issues on the workings of the group. Middle school and early high school groups are typically single-gender groups.

Working with Mandated and Involuntary Students

Many students are eager to participate in group counseling, and some students are reluctant to begin group counseling. Even when students can identify who wants them to receive help and why, they may not be interested in counseling at all. Some students are mandated to counseling for various reasons and have no choice about it. However, mandated students can, and often do, get significant benefits from counseling. The following are some tips for turning mandated students into active participants in group counseling.

Tips for the Mandated Student

   • Ask questions focused on what the mandated students will get out of the experience.
   • When students recognize that participating in counseling may get the referring party "off their backs," they generally are willing to establish counseling goals.

Integrating Students with Special Needs

We strongly believe that students with special needs can be included successfully in groups. SOS groups teach specific skills and competencies through psychoeducational activities. As you select students for group membership, pay attention to the competencies needed for the psychoeducational portions of the group. Often, activities can be selected that do not require a high level of academic ability, making the group an excellent setting for a diverse group of students. Some students with special needs have Individualized Education Plans that designate a prescribed amount of counseling as related services. When the defined objectives of the prescribed counseling are correlated to the development of social skills, group counseling is an especially appropriate setting.

Meeting the Needs of the Age Group

The needs of group members vary according to the developmental tasks of the age group (Malekoff, 2004). Group leaders of school-age children and adolescents must be aware of developmental needs that are related to age-appropriate peer-to-peer interaction (Kymissis & Halperin, 1996). Consider these guidelines to meet the developmental needs of students selected for groups:

Primary Groups
Students at this age enjoy groups that

- are activity based
- use simple language
- contain concrete examples
- allow for practice
- have short sessions

Intermediate Groups
Students at this age

- place a high value on processes that are fair

- can handle activities that are somewhat more academic
- are beginning to understand that others have different points of view

Middle School Groups

Students at this age

- are beginning to have the abilities to think abstractly, consider hypothetical situations, look at multiple dimensions of the same situation, and reflect on themselves
- feel the importance of social acceptance, and are at the peak of peer conformity

High School Groups

Students at this age

- benefit from opportunities for personal decision making
- can see multiple perspectives of a situation
- can think abstractly
- can work for longer group sessions

Special Confidentiality Considerations

Individual and group counseling are built upon the concepts of confidentiality and respect for the student's privacy. Confidentiality is an essential element in building the trust that is necessary for groups to do their work. The group agreement should contain clear language about maintaining confidentiality. Plan for how you will accomplish the following:

- Talk about confidentiality in the group with regard to the special challenges presented when there are more than two people in the room.
- Protect students from a level of disclosure that might result in embarrassment.
- Help students know how to share information about themselves and their experiences with their parents while still respecting the privacy of the other group members.
- Deal with breaches of confidentiality in the group.
- Decide how much to share with teachers, parents, and others about the group.

 See Appendix 4.A for several sample group agreements.

Organization and Management of Group Materials

All of the details of getting groups going in your school could be overwhelming without a good dose of organization from the very beginning. Here are some suggestions:

- Use a large binder or folder to contain everything related to setting up groups.
- Set up the following sections in the binder or folder:
  - —*Needs assessments.* Collect all of the returned needs assessments from teachers.
  - —*Groups.* Include the roster for the group, the points sheet for each member of the group, and six group session forms. Attach a library pocket onto the back of each roster and insert the parent response portion of the parent permission slip for each member of the group. Insert tabs or dividers for each SOS group you facilitate. Number or name the groups.
  - —*Forms.* Keep a master copy of each of the forms that you use in one section of the binder.
- Schedule all SOS groups to be on the same session number each week.
- During the fall semester, offer SOS groups for students in Grades 1, 3, and 5. Then, during the spring semester, offer SOS groups for students in Grades 2 and 4.
- Write case notes using the group session form.
- Use the students' goal folders as records of their progress in group. Using goal folders in this way creates a separate file for each member and protects confidentiality.

Accountability for SOS Groups

Providing group counseling is a key function of counselors in school settings. Therefore, it is crucial to be particularly effective in your accountability for these services (Loesch & Ritchie, 2005). Counselors can be fully accountable only to the extent that they generate substantive evidence that their activities have changed students in ways that are positive and desirable. The resulting changes need not be monumental; in fact, the changes are often small or subtle. However, the changes must be documented through an accountability activity and then made evident to appropriate stakeholders. There are many ways to demonstrate the benefits gained through participation in SOS groups. These include the following:

- Count the number of students who have participated and the number of group sessions held.

- Use rating scales and semistructured interviews to evaluate the effectiveness of the groups. This can include

  —creating a rating scale to use with students at the end of the group to measure the students' degree of satisfaction with participation in the activities.

  —conducting brief, semistructured interviews with teachers, parents, or students to determine what they found to be most helpful (Dennison, 1997).

  —using needs assessment forms to return to the referring teachers and ask for postgroup ratings on the original behaviors.

- Compare student data (such as discipline or attendance data) before and after group participation. Although issues are complex and are influenced by many factors other than group participation, data can be used to demostrate that SOS groups contribute to positive change.

- Calculate the percentage of students participating in SOS groups who achieved their goals. Be sure to present these data without listing the students' names.

- Show skills-achievement rates.

Summary

- Having referral sources who are thoroughly familiar with the SOS group work model will help encourage referrals.

- Implementing the SOS model requires some education and preparation for teachers, administrators, parents, and students. The result, though, is a perception of groups as useful, proactive, and effective, all of which will lead to stakeholders' assistance in referring students for groups.

- Logistics in the school require special consideration. In each school setting there are unique needs that can be resolved through collaboration.

- SOS groups incorporate all kinds of students and student needs into the mix. Membership inclusions and exclusions require thoughtful consideration.

- There are useful ways to organize group materials to save time.

- Goal folders and group session forms are useful for case notes.

- Remember that the first journey through this process will take some time, but once in place, the system will allow you to provide opportunities for many students to work on their goals and learn skills.

- Accountability is crucial. Select a method or methods to demonstrate the positive changes that occur in group.

APPENDIX 4.A

Forms for Implementing SOS Groups

Counselor Request Form

Group Agreement Elementary #1

Group Agreement K–12 #1

Group Agreement K–12 #2

Group Agreement Secondary #1

Group Agreement Secondary #2

Group Notes and Evaluation

Group Roster Sheet

Individual Group Diary

Informed Consent Form

Needs Assessment—Elementary

Needs Assessment—Elementary (filled in)

Needs Assessment—Middle School

Needs Assessment—High School

Needs Assessment—Student

Parent/Guardian Consent Form

Parent/Guardian Cover Letter

Points Sheet—Elementary

SOS Group Information Sheet for Faculty and Staff

SOS Group Information Sheet for Parents/Guardians

Counselor Request Form

_____ **School**

Guidance and Counseling Department—Counselor Request

To: _____

From: _____, Counselor

Date: _____

Please send _____ to ☐ Counseling Office at _____ A.M./P.M.

☐ Group Room # _____

☐ Other _____

_____ **School**

Guidance and Counseling Department—Counselor Request

To: _____

From: _____, Counselor

Date: _____

Please send _____ to ☐ Counseling Office at _____ A.M./P.M.

☐ Group Room # _____

☐ Other _____

_____ **School**

Guidance and Counseling Department—Counselor Request

To: _____

From: _____, Counselor

Date: _____

Please send _____ to ☐ Counseling Office at _____ A.M./P.M.

☐ Group Room # _____

☐ Other _____

_____ **School**

Guidance and Counseling Department—Counselor Request

To: _____

From: _____, Counselor

Date: _____

Please send _____ to ☐ Counseling Office at _____ A.M./P.M.

☐ Group Room # _____

☐ Other _____

Group Agreement

1. Be on time.

2. Follow directions.

3. Take turns speaking.

4. Listen and/or participate.

5. Speak kindly to all.

Group Agreement

Bring yourself to the group and nothing else.

Everyone gets an opportunity to share, including the leader.

You can skip your turn if you wish.

Listen to the person who is speaking.

There are no interruptions, put-downs, or gossip.

Share the time equally.

Stay in your own space.

Note. From *The Sharing Circle Handbook* (poster), by S. Palomares, S. Schuster, and C. Watkins, 1992, Austin, TX: PRO-ED, Inc. Copyright 1992 by PRO-ED, Inc. Adapted with permission.

Group Agreement

Be respectful and confidential.

Participate in group activities.

61

Stay in your own space.

Pay attention. Look at the speaker.

Pass if you choose.

Be supportive. No put-downs.

Wait for your turn to speak.

Note. From "Process/Group Agreements Poster" in *Belonging* (p. 37), by J. Devencenzi and S. Pendergast, 1999, Austin, TX: PRO-ED, Inc. Copyright 1999 by PRO-ED, Inc. Adapted with permission.

Group Agreement K–12 #2

Group Agreement

Everyone be quiet when someone is talking.

62 Respect one another.

Listen attentively.

Get everyone to talk.

Treat others the way you want to be treated.

Support others' ideas even if you disagree.

No dissing when someone is talking.

No cursing.

Note. From *Group Work with Adolescents* (p. 77), by A. Malekoff, 2004, New York: Guilford Press. Copyright 2004 by Guilford. Adapted with permission.

Group Agreement

Find something to talk about and _____ n it.

Contribute to the conversation of the group.

Think of something important to say.

Keep eye contact with all members.

Talk nicely, be friendly, and don't act like
an imbecile.

Make facial expressions when you speak
to make conversation more interesting.

Express yourself and make yourself clear.

Give other group members a chance
to contribute.

Try to find out the main idea of the
discussion.

One person speaks at a time.

I, _____, agree to follow these rules as best I can.

Signature: _____ Date: _____

Note. From *Group Work with Adolescents* (p. 76), by A. Malekoff, 2004, New York: Guilford Press. Copyright 2004 by Guilford.
Adapted with permission

Group Notes and Evaluation

SOS Group: _____ Session #: _____ Date: _____

Activity

64

Notes

Evaluation

The students:

Member initials	Present	Met the objective of the lesson	Identified a specific goal that is the presence of something rather than the absence of something	Scaled his or her current status	Committed to a task

The group leader:

	conveyed to the group members that they are trusted to help themselves
	maintained boundaries in the group
	used effective group leadership skills

Group Roster Sheet

_____ **School**

Guidance and Counseling

Group: _____ Grade: _____

Parent Permission Returned	Group Members		Sessions/Dates						
	First Name	Last Name	1	2	3	4	5	6	Booster

Individual Group Diary

Name: _____ Date: _____

My reason for coming here: _____
_____

I will know when things are better for me when I am able to: _____

66
_____

On the scale below, if 1 = *your problems are in complete control of you*, and 10 = *you are in complete control of your problems*, circle where you are today:

     1   2   3   4   5   6   7   8   9   10

Group Day #1

Where are you today on the scale? _____

What did you discover today about yourself that will help you move to a different point?

_____
_____

Group Day #2

Where are you today on the scale? _____

What did you discover today about yourself that will help you move to a different point?

_____
_____

Group Day #3

Where are you today on the scale? _____

What did you discover today about yourself that will help you move to a different point?

_____
_____

Group Day #4

Where are you today on the scale? _____

What did you discover today about yourself that will help you move to a different point?

_____

_____

Group Day #5

Where are you today on the scale? _____

What did you discover today about yourself that will help you move to a different point?

_____

_____

Group Day #6

Where are you today on the scale? _____

What did you discover today about yourself that will help you move to a different point?

_____

_____

Individual Group Diary

SOS Group

SOS groups at our school use solution-focused approaches to help students establish their own goals for improvement. In the group we will learn skills to understand ourselves, communicate with others, show responsibility in our behavior, resolve conflicts, make decisions, and take care of ourselves. Some important points about SOS groups include:

1. The group is based on maintaining confidentiality. An exception to confidentiality exists when the leader has concerns that a group member is in danger of being hurt or hurting someone else.

2. We insure that all students are shown respect and support.

3. Sudents are expected to take turns talking and let everyone have a chance to talk.

4. Students have the right to pass, or not comment, on things that are discussed.

I have read and understand the description of the SOS group,

Name of Student: _____ Grade: _____

Signature of Student: _____ Date: _____

_____ **School**

Guidance and Counseling Program

To: _____ Grade: _____

From: _____ Date: _____

Re: SOS Group Referrals

This semester I will lead SOS groups for students in your grade level. These groups are designed to teach students a process to identify their goals and specific skills to be able to reach their goals. You may have students with these concerns:

a. attendance

b. school attitudes and behaviors

c. peer relationships

d. study skills

e. being new to school

f. death of a family member or friend

g. family divorce

h. harassment issues

i. severe stress

j. other: _____

69

Please list the top 4 students in your class who could benefit from being in an SOS group and the letter for their issue of concern:

Please rate on a scale of 0 to 10, with 0 being the worst and 10 being the best, the student's behavior in these areas:

Student's Name	Issue	Knows and Accepts Self	Communicates with Peers and Adults	Takes Responsibility for Own Behavior	Makes Decisions Wisely	Resolves Conflict Nonviolently	Manages Self Well
I. _____							
II. _____							
III. _____							
IV. _____							

Please list the days of the week and times during the day when students from your class may participate in group:

_____

☐ I have no referrals for SOS Group at this time.

Thanks for returning this form to me via my mailbox by _____

_____Martin Elementary_____ **School**

Guidance and Counseling Program

To: **A. Williams**_____ Grade: **3**_____

From: **L. Smith**_____ Date: **9/1/2006**_____

Re: SOS Group Referrals

This semester I will lead SOS groups for students in your grade level. These groups are designed to teach students a process to identify their goals and specific skills to be able to reach their goals. You may have students with these concerns:

    a. attendance

    b. school attitudes and behaviors

    c. peer relationships

    d. study skills

    e. being new to school

    f. death of a family member or friend

    g. family divorce

    h. harassment issues

    i. severe stress

    j. other: _____

Please list the top 4 students in your class who could benefit from being in an SOS group and the letter for their issue of concern:

Please rate on a scale of 0 to 10, with 0 being the worst and 10 being the best, the student's behavior in these areas:

Student's Name	Issue	Knows and Accepts Self	Communicates with Peers and Adults	Takes Responsibility for Own Behavior	Makes Decisions Wisely	Resolves Conflict Nonviolently	Manages Self Well
I. Jeremy Johnson	c	4	3	6	5	7	3
II. Kelsey Rucker	a	3	4	6	5	7	2
III. Eric Hamilton	e	4	4	2	3	1	3
IV. Tamara Jefferson	b	4	4	4	5	5	3

Please list the days of the week and times during the day when students from your class may participate in group:

Tuesdays and Thursdays from 2:00–3:00_____

☐ I have no referrals for SOS Group at this time.

Thanks for returning this form to me via my mailbox by _____

Needs Assessment—Elementary (filled in)

_____ **School**

Guidance and Counseling Program

To: _____   Date: _____

From: _____

Re: SOS Group Referrals

This semester I will lead SOS groups for students. These groups teach students a process to identify their goals and specific skills to reach their goals. The groups will run for six weeks and will be rotated through the class periods. You may have students with these concerns:

a. School adjustment problems

b. Separation/divorce issues

c. Personal responsibility issues

d. Social skills needs

e. Anger issues

f. Depression issues

g. Fear/anxiety issues

h. Abuse or trauma issues

i. School motivation issues

j. Other: _____

71

Please list the top 2 students in your classes who could benefit from being in an SOS group and the letter for their issue of concern:

Please rate on a scale of 0 to 10, with 0 being the worst and 10 being the best, the student's behavior in these areas:

Student's Name and Class Period	Issue	Knows and Accepts Self	Communicates with Peers and Adults	Takes Responsibility for Own Behavior	Makes Decisions Wisely	Resolves Conflict Nonviolently	Manages Self Well
I. _____							
II. _____							

Please list the days of the week when students from your classes may participate in group:

_____

☐ I have no referrals for SOS Group at this time.

Thanks for returning this form to me via my mailbox by _____

_____ **High School**

Guidance and Counseling Program

To: _____   Date: _____

From: _____

Re: SOS Group Referrals

This semester I will lead SOS groups for students. These groups teach students a process to identify their goals and specific skills to reach their goals. The groups will run for six weeks and will be rotated through the class periods. You may have students with these concerns:

72

a. Stress management

b. Family relationship issues

c. Personal responsibility issues

d. Conflict resolution issues

e. Truancy

f. Depression issues

g. Fear/anxiety issues

h. Abuse or trauma issues

i. Academic achievement/school motivation issues

j. Other: _____

Please list the top 2 students in your classes who could benefit from being in an SOS group and the letter for their issue of concern:

		Please rate on a scale of 0 to 10, with 0 being the worst and 10 being the best, the student's behavior in these areas:					
Student's Name and Class Period	**Issue**	Knows and Accepts Self	Communicates with Peers and Adults	Takes Responsibility for Own Behavior	Makes Decisions Wisely	Resolves Conflict Nonviolently	Manages Self Well
I. _____							
II. _____							

Please list the days of the week when students from your classes may participate in group:

_____

☐ I have no referrals for SOS Group at this time.

Thanks for returning this form to me via my mailbox by _____

_____ **School**

Guidance and Counseling Program

Name: _____

Grade: _____ Date: _____

This year we will have SOS groups for students in your grade level. These groups are designed to help students identify their goals and gain specific skills to be able to reach their goals. This survey is to find out if you are interested in being in a group at our school. Place an X in the box before a topic if you have concerns about any of the topics below and would like to be in a group.

Return your form to _____. **73**

- ☐ attendance
- ☐ school attitudes and behaviors
- ☐ peer relationships
- ☐ study skills
- ☐ being new to school
- ☐ death of a family member or friend
- ☐ family divorce
- ☐ harassment issues
- ☐ severe stress
- ☐ other: _____

A question I have for my counselor is: _____

_____

_____

_____.

Parent/Guardian Consent Form

I, _____, understand that my son/daughter, _____, has been selected to participate in an SOS Group at _____ School. I have received information about the group and by signing below, give consent for my child to participate.

74

I understand that the group counseling program is offered to students in an effort to provide an enriching and productive learning environment for students. I understand that my child is responsible for completing any class work that he or she misses while attending group sessions.

My child has permission to participate in an SOS Group scheduled to run from _____ to _____.

_____   _____
Parent/Guardian Signature   Date

Please return this form to _____ by _____.

_____ **School**

Guidance and Counseling Program

Dear Parent or Guardian,

Your son/daughter, _____, has requested to attend the SOS Group

at our school. The times for this group will be _____ on _____ (day) from

_____ to _____.

    The purpose of the SOS group is to assist students in a confidential group setting with identifying

their strengths and abilities to solve their own concerns. In addition, students will further their skills in the

areas of self-knowledge and self-acceptance, interpersonal communication, responsible behavior, conflict

resolution, decision making, and self-care.

    Your permission for your son/daughter to participate will be appreciated. Please feel free to contact

your son's/daughter's teacher, _____, with questions about referral,

or contact _____, counselor, with questions about the group.

Please return by _____.

Thanks!

_____, School Counselor

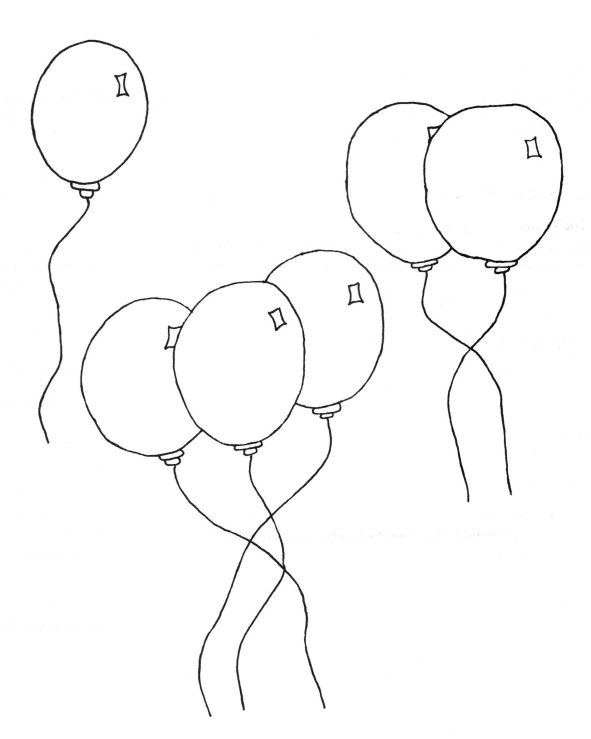

76

SOS Groups

The solution-focused SOS group program is specifically designed to help students in school settings. The letters *SOS* are used to refer to "Strengthened Sense of Self." SOS is also associated with an emergency call for help. Some students are referred to SOS groups because of a life crisis of some kind, and others are referred simply to receive help in making positive changes.

Focus of the Groups

The focus of the group program is achieving positive goals with students. Group leaders link the benefits of the group setting with solution-focused approaches to help students identify their strengths and abilities to solve their concerns. Groups meet at school for six weeks. During each group session students will learn important skills to help them be successful. In group, these skills will be tailored to address individual student needs and concerns.

Skills Topics

- Self-Knowledge and Acceptance—Students will learn about their abilities, interests, and personal characteristics. When students learn to identify their strengths and the areas in which they need to improve, their sense of self is strengthened.

- Interpersonal and Communication Skills—Students will develop positive interpersonal relationships and communications skills to promote positive interactions with each other. Students will also learn to value differences and uniqueness among people.

- Responsible Behavior and Personal Responsibility—Students will develop personal responsibility for their behavior. They will learn how attitudes and perceptions can affect behavior, how feelings and behaviors are related to goals and consequences, and how behavior can be changed.

- Conflict Resolution—Students will learn nonviolent ways to resolve conflicts. Students will also learn styles of cooperative behavior and healthy expressions of anger.

- Decision Making—Students will learn the steps for making effective decisions. They will also learn the factors that influence change and decision making. Emphasis will be placed on responsibility and individual choice.

- Self-Care and Self-Management—Students will learn how to express feelings in healthy ways, advocate for themselves, manage their time, and manage stress.

SOS Groups

Focus of the Groups

The focus of the group program is achieving positive goals with students. Group leaders link the benefits of the group setting with solution-focused approaches to help students identify their strengths and abilities to solve their concerns. Groups meet at school for six weeks. During each group session students will learn important skills to help them be successful. In group, these skills will be tailored to address individual student needs and concerns.

78

Skills Topics

- Self-Knowledge and Acceptance—Students will learn about their abilities, interests, and personal characteristics. When students learn to identify their strengths and the areas in which they need to improve, their sense of self is strengthened.

- Interpersonal and Communication Skills—Students will develop positive interpersonal relationships and communications skills to promote positive interactions with each other. Students will also learn to value differences and uniqueness among people.

- Responsible Behavior and Personal Responsibility—Students will develop personal responsibility for their behavior. They will learn how attitudes and perceptions can affect behavior, how feelings and behaviors are related to goals and consequences, and how behavior can be changed.

- Conflict Resolution—Students will learn nonviolent ways to resolve conflicts. Students will also learn styles of cooperative behavior and healthy expressions of anger.

- Decision Making—Students will learn the steps for making effective decisions. They will also learn the factors that influence change and decision making. Emphasis will be placed on responsibility and individual choice.

- Self-Care and Self-Management—Students will learn how to express feelings in healthy ways, advocate for themselves, manage their time, and manage stress.

5 Getting Kids Ready for Group

Interviewing for Solutions

Setting Goals with the Solution-Focused Process

Placing the Student in Group

Interviewing for Solutions

Our initial contacts with students, parents, and teachers are important. The conversations we have with students can strongly influence the way they view themselves and their problems. Solution-focused counseling is a shift from a focus on problems and deficits to a search for competencies and strengths in order to develop solutions (Bertolino & Schultheis, 2002). The active search for solutions begins with the very first contact regarding a school problem and is based on the assumption that it is easier to increase existing successes and competencies, no matter how small, than it is to eliminate problems.

Screening for Group

Some students show up with the idea that they are coming to talk about being in a group. With others, we bring up the idea that being in a group would be helpful to them. One way to introduce the topic is to watch for opportunities during the initial interview to honestly say something to the effect that "being in a group would be a good way to work on _____ (fill in the blank)." Through the screening process you may decide not to place the student in a group, but if you do, you have laid the groundwork.

Screening for SOS groups is incorporated in the initial solution-focused interview. We hold the following three questions in mind: (a) Is there any reason this student should not be in a group? (b) Will this student benefit from SOS group work? (c) Will this student be able to participate productively in the SOS group and not interfere with individual members' and the group's ability to carry on its work?

Our first screening question is, "Is there any reason this student should not be in a group?" In Chapter 4 we detailed specific reasons why group work is not the modality of choice for some kids. Once we have ruled out the clear cases for not including a kid in a group, we still have to stay in an exploratory position regarding a particular student and group work. We use the second and third questions to arrive at a decision.

"Will this student benefit from SOS group work?" is the next question. For example, if a withdrawn kid is referred, initially it would appear that he or she would benefit from the opportunity to develop relationships in a group. Our next question might be, "Does this kid, at this point, have enough of an ability to interact to make use of group relationships?"

Once we have determined that a student could benefit potentially from being in an SOS group, we ask the third question: "Will this student be able to participate in the SOS group in such a way as to not interfere with the group's purpose and with other members' progress?" Again having ruled out the extreme cases, we stay curious. Consider the student who has not been identified as having a disability but has been referred for difficulty with impulse control in the classroom. Kids learn to control their impulses in groups, so it would seem reasonable to further explore the idea of group placement. During the interview process we gather information and observe to determine if, in our opinion, the student has so much difficulty with impulse control that teaching the concept of sharing would take up too much of the group's time. It might be that this kid needs some one-on-one time before entering a group. On the other hand, we might see over the course of the interview, that the kid has calmed and his responses become more reflective and less reactive. At this point we might decide that with direction and the structure of an SOS group, the child would benefit from being in a group without being a detriment to the group.

It is important to acknowledge that we all make mistakes in group placements. Mistakes almost always can be used as opportunities for teaching problem solving in a group.

We invite you to use the following exercise as practice in screening for group. Explore the question of whether an SOS group would be a good way to help this student.

 ## AN EXERCISE IN SCREENING FOR GROUP

Joseph was referred by his sixth-grade teacher because he seemed sad most of the time. The counselor, Mrs. Larkin, stood when Joseph came in the office. She attempted to make eye contact with him and was able to, just briefly, as she showed him where to sit. Mrs. Larkin sat beside him and asked Joseph if he knew why it had been suggested that they have a talk. He shook his head but did not look up. She asked if he thought there was anything that she could help him with and he shook his head "no." Mrs. Larkin then asked Joseph what he had been doing the last time he had some fun. At this point Joseph looked up and almost smiled. He told her about his room at home and the games that he played when he was alone. He could not remember any time when he had fun with anyone else.

 ## Exercise

Think about Joseph as a potential group member. Using the three questions for screening for group, ask yourself, "At this point would I recommend SOS group work for Joseph?"

In Joseph's case we would be assessing whether he needed more one-on-one time and if he was too withdrawn to make use of group. We also need to continue to consider if it would take too much of the leader's time during group to keep him involved. Given his level of social withdrawal and possible depression, one place to continue to explore the question of group placement would be observing how capable Joseph is of engaging in the solution-focused process in the interview.

Guidelines for Developing an Alliance for Change

Our first task in the initial solution-focused interview is to form an alliance for change with the student. When the student walks into the office, we communicate that we are aligned with him or her and are curious to know how we can be helpful. Working to shift ownership of the problem to the student, we ask questions to assist with defining the referral problem in his or her own words and ideas. To be successful in helping the student, we must come to a shared, clear definition of the problem that can be stated behaviorally, again using the kid's words and ideas. The message we want to send to students is that *they* have the answers.

The following guidelines are designed to develop an alliance for change that includes mutual clarity and the student's ownership of the problem.

- The watchwords at our initial meeting are "respect" and "curiosity." Whatever your system is for making kids feel at ease, important, and valued, follow that system!

- We start by *acknowledging* the problem in a way that students can feel heard regarding their perspectives. The objective is to get a detailed behavioral picture, using questions that are geared toward defining the kids' problems, in their own words. A danger is using *our* words, so careful active listening is required. We work to match their language. The "video-talk" technique (Murphy, 1997) is one in which the student is encouraged to describe the problem as if he or she were doing a play-by-play of what exactly happens when the problem occurs. This technique can be quite informative regarding the student's point of view. Once we have this information, we can use the student's words and ideas regarding the problem.

- We listen for four kinds of "stories" that will hamper change: (a) blame stories, (b) impossibility stories, (c) invalidation stories, and (d) nonaccountability stories (O'Hanlon, 1999). Definitions of these problem stories and help with changing them are found in the next sections.

- We continue to *clarify* once we have the student's definition. We stay curious by using more questions to get details, such as, "When does the problem occur? Are others involved? Are there predictable events that occur with the problem?"

- With a picture in mind of what is going on from the students' perspective, the next step is to find out what efforts they have made in the past to resolve these difficulties and whether any of the efforts have paid off in any way. We are specifically looking for *strengths* and *exceptions* to the problems that can be used to make changes. We ask questions such as, "When in the past has the problem *not* occurred? How were you able to avoid the problem that time?" As we work with the students to find strengths, it is important to explicitly name the strengths.

• The final step is crucial to a positive outcome. Questions are geared toward determining to what extent kids see the problems as theirs to solve, that there is a need for change, and that the newly defined problem is within their capacity to change. After you have the answers to these questions, you may have to return to step one with a new definition of the problem, or you may be able to move on to goal setting.

↳ **See Appendix 5.A for examples of solution-focused, goal-setting language to use with specific problems.**

Recognizing Problem Stories

There are four kinds of stories that hamper change and require us to challenge ideas. Our goals are to listen, remain aligned with the kids, and assist students with listening to their own stories in a new way that has them take ownership of the problem. O'Hanlon (1999) described the stories as follows:

• *Blame stories* are focused on someone being wrong or bad, and who causes the current problem. Students may blame themselves or some other person. Examples of ideas in blame stories are: *I'm lazy and don't get my work done. She is too strict and won't let me say a word. The television is always on, so I can't concentrate.* Blame ideas do not invite change and can actively interfere with the change process.

• *Impossibility stories* suggest that change is impossible. They come from beliefs that the student has no power to change anything about the problem. The problem is seen as persistent, long lasting, pervasive, and inescapable. This view becomes self-fulfilling. Examples of these ideas are: *I'm ADD and everyone knows I can't do this kind of schoolwork. I'm "hyper" and I can't stay in my seat. Other kids don't like me and I'll never be able to have friends.*

• *Invalidation stories* involve decisions that the student's own or someone else's feelings, thoughts, desires, or personality is wrong or unacceptable. Examples of these ideas are: *I'm too sensitive. I need to just let this go and move on. I want to go to college, but that's a stupid idea.*

• *Nonaccountability stories* excuse students from responsibility for their actions by claiming that the cause of the problem is something out of their control. Nonaccountability ideas suggest that students have no choice regarding their actions and no ability to make any difference in what happens. Examples of these ideas are: *I come from a violent family, so I hit when I'm angry. Everybody I know cusses ... that's why I cuss.*

Challenging Problem Stories

The following guidelines are useful in changing these four kinds of problem stories into solutions (O'Hanlon, 1999):

- Actively elicit more specific details regarding the problem, asking questions that provide counterevidence that does not fit with the story. Students will often free themselves from old interpretations or beliefs by simply engaging in conversation about the problem.
- Create a situation during the interview that challenges the story directly. An example would be when kids say, "I can't sit still." Bring their attention to the fact that they have been sitting still while we have been talking.
- Ask the student to describe the experience and facts. Validate the past problematic points of view, but add a twist that softens the circumstances or adds a sense of possibility.
- Focus exploration on the student's strengths, reminding the kid that he or she is more than "a problem."
- Reframe the story, creating a compassionate and more benevolent interpretation.

Practicing Interviewing for Solutions

Murphy (1997) gave a thorough description of the interviewing-for-solutions process. It is important to note that in the solution-focused approach the first interview might well be the only meeting; through the interview process the kid may come up with solutions to the problem, take ownership, and make the change. The following are three examples of teacher referrals. We suggest that you use them as opportunities to practice interviewing for solutions.

 INTERVIEWING: EXAMPLE 1

Dominick was referred for group counseling because of his difficulty getting along with his peers. His fourth-grade teacher, Ms. Jones, was primarily concerned with Dominick's deteriorating class performance. When he came in for an initial interview, the counselor, Mr. Smith, did everything he could to make Dominick feel welcome and at ease, including smiling, making good eye contact, and taking a seat close to him.

Mr. Smith introduced himself and said that Ms. Jones thought that he might be helpful to Dominick. He asked Dominick if he knew why his teacher had suggested that they speak. Dominick looked at the floor and shook his head. Mr. Smith then gave a brief description of what Ms. Jones had told him, but finished by saying that he wanted to hear from Dominick what he thought about this problem. Dominick looked up for a second and said, "Some guys pick on me." The counselor then asked Dominick to pretend that what happened was in a movie and to tell him exactly what went on from start to finish. Dominick gladly took up this challenge, detailing how several boys would start pulling on his backpack as he walked down the hall until his backpack would fall on the floor. He said that then they would pick it up and keep it away from him, making him late for class.

Let's consider the dilemmas facing Mr. Smith and Dominick. Mr. Smith has a possible bullying situation to sort out, but at this moment he is sitting with a kid who has a problem, blames others, and has no idea how to help himself. Dominick's school performance is suffering and he sees himself as having no part in the difficulties he is experiencing.

Exercise

Put yourself in Mr. Smith's position with Dominick. Using the solution-focused approach and the guidelines presented earlier, decide what steps you would take to get more details regarding the situation and write them down. You might be tempted to skip the "writing down" part, but we encourage you to do the writing. Getting specific and being disciplined with our use of language are keys to internalizing the SOS approach and being successful with kids.

Looking at what you have written, did you remember to repeat what you had heard in Dominick's words? This step is important in acknowledging his thoughts and giving him the idea that you are on his side. Asking questions that challenge the blame story while remaining aligned with Dominick are necessary. You would need to pinpoint any times when these events have not happened on the way to class or when Dominick had positive experiences with his classmates. His responses clarify and define his strengths and exceptions to the problem.

 ## INTERVIEWING: EXAMPLE 2

Sophie, a seventh grader, had missed at least 2 days of school every week for more than a month. Her attendance had been quite satisfactory in the past. School records indicated that she was a good student with above-average intelligence. In the initial interview with the counselor, Mrs. Wright, Sophie detailed her parents' divorce and a move to her mother's boyfriend's house. Mrs. Wright determined with questions that Sophie understood that her absences were a problem. Sophie described what mornings were like in her new home and what happened on the days that she was able to catch the bus. Sophie's definition of the problem was that her mother did not care about her since the divorce. Mrs. Wright decided from listening to Sophie that she had good problem-solving abilities.

Mrs. Wright now faces the challenge that Sophie's definition of her problem does not match the school's concerns. Mrs. Wright might well have to address the school absences through other channels while she works with Sophie on the problem Sophie has defined.

Exercise

Using the solution-focused approach, what language would you use in your effort to shift Sophie into an ownership position with this problem? Again, write down what you would say and the questions you would ask.

Here we would have to back up and get details about the problem as Sophie sees it. We would need to identify with Sophie's experience, so that our questions and language would acknowledge Sophie and clarify the situation as she experienced it. We would no longer be talking about school absences. Sophie has defined a problem, and we would be looking for her strengths and for exceptions to the problem. There would be a specific need to determine if Sophie was seeing the problem as impossible to solve. If so, we would work to challenge that idea. We would have to determine what Sophie believed she had the power to change in the situation. If she did not believe that she had the power to change any part of this, we would have to work with her to define the problem within the boundaries of what she could change herself.

INTERVIEWING: EXAMPLE 3

Brianna was referred by her teacher because of the problems she had getting along with her third-grade classmates. She was very bright but used her good mind to make fun of others too often. Other kids were hurt and complained about her. Brianna did not see any problem, except that she wanted to have friends. She knew that her teacher was disturbed by the behavior that Brianna defined as "joking."

Exercise

As Brianna's counselor, what questions would you ask to shift this situation to one that she could own? What specifics would you work to bring to light?

To help Brianna we would be looking for her strengths, a determination of when she had had friends in the past, what her history of making and keeping friends was, and changes in her friendship patterns for which she could take ownership. You have to keep in mind that Brianna does not see "making fun" of others as a problem at this time. The important question of "How would your life be better if _____ was no longer a problem?" can be very helpful with kids' taking ownership. In this case the question might be "How would your life be better if _____ was not upset with you about this 'joking'?" As always, we stay with the student's language regarding the problem.

Mandated Counseling

When students are mandated to come to counseling, we pay specific attention to "meeting" them as we identify areas for change. Special care is given to matching language with these students. Working toward ownership of problems will often require questioning aimed at improvement that others want. Since these students may not see the problems that have them mandated to counseling as their problems, our questions are geared toward how to improve their lives by having important others be "happier" with them. Examples of questions would be "What would they have to see you doing differently to get them off your back?" or "What will be the first signal to them that they can get off your back?" With students mandated to counseling and in a situation like Brianna's, in which she does not see the behavior as a problem, exploring the impact of having important adults upset with them can reframe a problem and assist kids with taking ownership.

Setting Goals with the Solution-Focused Approach

It is essential to establish a clear picture of what the solution looks like in the eyes of the student. Positive change is enhanced when practitioners "begin with the end in mind" by clarifying goals at the outset (Murphy, 1997). Outcome research indicates that success is greatly enhanced when counselors obtain a clear idea of what people want from counseling, and accommodate these goals throughout the counseling process (Marmar, Horowitz, Weiss, & Marziali, 1986; Orlinsky, Grawe, & Parks, 1994).

From Problem to Goal

The success of a member's SOS group experience depends largely on the goal-setting process. Once the problem has been defined in such a way that the student can take ownership, our task is to collaboratively define a change that will have meaning for that student. This leap is not always easy. The change that has meaning for the adults involved does not necessarily have meaning for the child. We have to look at what our tolerance is for the student's definition of the problem and corresponding goals versus the referring source's or other adults' definitions and goals. Where there is a significant difference in definitions, the groundwork we do with colleagues and parents will pay off. Ongoing clear communication and education of colleagues and parents are essentials (Webb, 1999).

The leadership task is to stay with the process and with the awareness that the student has the answers. We make use of the information we have already gathered about the kid's strengths, the exceptions to the problem, previous efforts to solve this problem, and the kid's ownership of the need to change. Staying curious and exploratory, we ask questions and listen. In great part our success is determined by our abilities to make those questions open-ended and to not create an agenda. Asking questions in the solution-focused process is intended to lead kids to new ways of thinking and to increased senses of their abilities to solve problems. In preparing students for SOS group work *we begin to teach the goal-setting process* as we collaboratively frame observable and attainable goals. We do this by emphasizing each aspect of effective goal setting and supporting the effort that the student makes.

Essential Elements of Effective Goals

Goals first need to be *specific*. For example, the goal "I want my mother to respect me" is not specific. The goal "When I walk in the house and see my mother, I will make eye contact and smile at her" is specific. Asking more detailed questions is the best technique for establishing specific goals. A helpful question is "What will you be doing differently when this is no longer a problem?"

To be effective a goal should be a *small step*. "Mary will stop having arguments with her friend Shelley" requires too many steps to be one goal. "Mary will wear the bracelet her grandmother gave her each day for a week to remind her to smile when she sees Shelley" could be a goal for Mary. Questions like, "What will be the first sign that _____ (problem) has improved?" lead to goals that are small steps.

Scaling is a useful tool to invite the student to think about the present situation in specifics and send the message that we expect measurable progress. Scaling questions can be framed in a number of ways. The basic format is "On a scale of one to ten, with one being the worst this situation could be and ten being the best the situation could be, what number describes where the situation is today?" For example, we might ask Mary from the example above, "On a scale of one to ten, with one being the worst and ten being the best, what number would you give your friendship with Shelley right now?" We might also ask what number she thinks Shelley would give the friendship. Scaling can become a part of the goal when students are asked to say what they want the number to be by a certain date.

In establishing goals an additional scaling question can be helpful, such as, "How confident are you on a scale of one to ten, with one being the least confident and ten being the most confident, that you can reach the goal, or goals, that you have set?" The answer to this question might require that the goal be modified. Scaling is used in solution-focused work to evaluate, modify goals, or create new goals. In SOS group work we use scaling during check-in to help kids evaluate their progress.

Goals should be stated in *positive terms* that represent the presence of something rather than the absence of something. "Gabriel will not start fights" is a goal, but probably will not interfere with Gabriel's fighting. On the playground Gabriel will remember to count to ten when he feels angry at least five times during the next week" has potential to interrupt a pattern of behavior. Stating goals in positive terms gives direction. Questions that lead to what the kid *will* be doing rather than what he or she will *not* be doing lead to solutions.

Goals must be *meaningful* and *relevant* to the student to be effective. "Eddie will do his assigned social studies reading next week" may be a very meaningful goal to the adults in Eddie's environment, but not to him, yet. "Eddie will ask his mother to sit with him for thirty minutes while he reads his social studies assignment" will have meaning for him if his goal is to have more time with his mother. Note that if making the adults "happy" is the only opening that has meaning for Eddie, we would use it.

It can be difficult to define goals with students, mandated or otherwise, who are being referred for reasons with which they do not agree. Murphy (1997) suggested that an approach that can be helpful in finding a meaningful goal with kids who feel unfairly treated is wondering with them "What kinds of things would prove them wrong about you?" Table 2.1 provides good information regarding Murphy's guidelines for goal setting.

 ## GOAL SETTING: EXAMPLE 1

Anthony, who had been referred for poor classroom participation, had worked with the counselor to define his problem. He wanted to talk with other kids at recess and to have someone to sit with in the lunchroom.

 ## Exercise

What questions would you ask to help Anthony to establish a goal? What would define an effective goal for Anthony? Write down the details of your process of assisting Anthony with establishing a goal.

We should be concerned with staying with Anthony's definition of the change that he wants and with using language appropriate for Anthony's level of maturity. Defining the specifics must be about his ideas. Asking questions that make use of his strengths and exceptions to the problem will assist in defining the small, positive steps he can take to meet the goal that has meaning for him. Again, questions that focus on how he will know when this is no longer a problem will lead him to specific goals.

This situation represents another of those in which the referring source has a goal different from the student's. Choosing to place Anthony in a group will give the counselor the unique opportunity to gather information about Anthony's difficulties that she can make use of to assist the teacher.

 ## GOAL SETTING: EXAMPLE 2

Lilianna was referred by several of her teachers because she talked throughout their classes and resisted complying with requests to stop talking. The counselor determined in the initial interview that Lilianna could control herself and that there had been a great deal of recent disruption in her home life. As the counselor asked for details of what was happening in class, Lilianna took ownership of the fact that she was causing herself trouble by talking "too much."

 ## Exercise

As Lilianna's counselor, what questions would you ask her to move the problem she has defined to a goal? Remember to consider all the elements that you will need to keep in mind as you write down your thoughts.

As with Anthony, the task would be to find a small, specific step that represents something that Lilianna would be doing that would be meaningful to her. We would again be asking about exceptions and using her strengths. The scaling question of how confident she felt about making the change would give us important information. Depending on her response, we could proceed or revise the goal to one that she felt more confident she could achieve.

Students with Unrealistic Goals

There are times when the goals that are meaningful to kids are unrealistic. These include goals that are not possible or require other people to make changes. Such situations are difficult to negotiate, but they are not impossible. Setting a realistic goal may require quite a bit of reflecting on the "wish." We work to remain empathic rather than challenging and look for what the need is under the wish. Questions we might ask are "What difference would it make in your life now, when that occurs?" or "How will it feel when that happens, and how would it change your life? What is appealing about that?" Answers to these questions or others like them will lead to doable goals.

 ### GOAL SETTING: EXAMPLE 3

> Simon's grandfather had died two months before Simon was referred. His mother asked that the counselor see him because Simon was resisting going to school. In the counselor's office Simon defined his problem as the loss of his grandfather. The goal that had meaning for him was that his grandfather would be alive.

 ## Exercise

> *Simon has an unrealistic goal. What questions would you ask him to help him define an attainable goal? How would your questions differ, depending on his maturity level?*

Our first challenge would be to respond to the unrealistic goal and discover what it is that Simon is missing that he had when his grandfather was alive. Once we had more information about the changes that his grandfather's death had brought, we would be in a position to help him define a step that he could take to replace something that was lost. Use of language might be the most significant difference that maturity level would make.

By the time you and the student have set a goal, you are ready to decide (a) that you and the student have completed your work together, (b) that you will work with him or her individually, *or* (c) that you are ready to proceed with group placement.

 See Appendix 5.B for a helpful Solution-Focused Interview Guide.

Placing the Student in Group

Once the student has a defined goal and meets the suitability tests for group inclusion, it is time to consider the benefits of inclusion in a group. Some important tasks can be accomplished in the session that will prepare the student to participate successfully in group.

Joining a Group with a Goal

Potential group members need the specific details of when and where the group meets, and the length and number of sessions. If we have not done so already, we provide a description of the group. Using developmentally appropriate language we explain that several students will be getting together to help one another solve their problems. We then introduce the concept that a number of kids working on their goals together can give *all* kids more ideas and strategies for solving their problems and the incentive to keep trying.

The student may have questions. There may be resistance to the idea of being in a group. The more confident we are in the benefits of group, the easier it is to engage the kid in the undertaking. No matter how confident and enthusiastic we are, however, there are kids who adamantly do not want to be in a group. It is our belief that anyone who is in this position should not be forced to join a group.

Goal Folder

The goal that has come out of the solution-focused process is written out, either by us or by the student, depending on maturity level. Along with the goal, we include scaling forms in the SOS group work folder. We describe check-in and let the student know that we will ask the scaling question at the beginning of each session to evaluate progress. It is a valuable practice to ask the students to rate their current status relative to their goals. The emphasis is on the fact that the purpose of the group is positive change.

Informed Consent

Informed consent must be pursued actively with potential group members. Students must be informed about the group and its processes in words they can understand. The essential element of informed consent defines the limits of confidentiality. We must make it clear to students that we will not share their secrets unless we have specific concerns that they may cause harm to themselves or someone else.

 See Appendix 4.A for a sample informed consent form.

Group Agreements

In Chapter 3 we introduced the importance of the use of clear agreements that create the boundaries for member participation. Group agreements, or rules, define what is expected of members as part of a group. Agreements provide the basis for the group to carry on its business. An example of an agreement might be "Only one person speaks at a time." In this agreement we establish a boundary that says, It is safe to speak; what you have to say will be heard; and every voice is valued. Group agreements outline the group culture we want to promote.

Some group leaders choose to develop agreements collaboratively with their group members; this can be especially useful with adolescents. Others establish a list of agreements that they talk about with potential group members before they join a group. Time constraints and the maturity level of the group often dictate this latter choice, but either method can be effective. Whether you decide to consider member input or provide the group with an established list, we again suggest that you consider the agreements as guidelines for group involvement rather than laws to be enforced. On the other hand, violations of agreements should be noted in group and the discussion of the violations must be used for the benefit of the group and the member or members who violated the agreements. We, as leaders, have the opportunity to model healthy self-expression and to create trust when we make agreements explicit and process violations of agreements as a group.

Using developmentally appropriate language, include these basic agreements: (a) Attend group each time for the whole time, (b) take a fair share of time, and (c) agree to confidentiality. Confidentiality always receives special emphasis and, again, is discussed in different ways, depending on maturity level.

If agreements are established by the leader rather than developed with the group, it is recommended that they be discussed at the initial interview and again at the first meeting of the group. Development of agreements with the group occurs at the beginning of the first SOS group meeting. With younger students particularly, group agreements can be posted where the group can see them as a reminder. You may choose to have new group members sign group agreements and include them in the group work folder.

 We include examples of group agreements for different levels of maturity in Appendix 4.A.

Tips for Group Agreements

- Elementary students can earn points at the end of each group session for following the rules. Points can be traded for something tangible when the roup ends.

- When group agreements are posted where the group can see them, often just a gesture toward the appropriate rule is a sufficient reminder.

- If members are involved in creating agreements, limit the number. Younger students can get overenthusiastic about this activity.

- Some leaders include group rules in a group agreement form for members to sign.

- Remember to process as a group any perceived violations of the group agreements. This is a great opportunity to model self-expression in an assertive way.

Summary

- We use the initial interview to help screen for group placement and to educate about group work. There are three questions we use in exploring the question of a group placement.

- In the initial interview we work to create an alliance for change using open-ended questions intended to shift the definition and ownership of the problem to the kid.

- Using the solution-focused approach, we define the kid's strengths and exceptions to his or her difficulties to assist with goal setting.

- There are four kinds of problem stories that are always challenged in solution-focused interviewing.

- When students have unrealistic goals, ask questions to find the meaning behind these unrealistic goals.

- Clear goals that are specific, small steps and that are positive, relevant, and meaningful to the kid are the bases for successful group experience.

- After a decision is reached to place the student in an SOS group, we give the student specific information, including informed consent.

- An SOS group folder includes the kid's goal and group agreements. The group agreements, or rules, form the basis for how the group carries on its business.

Interviewing for Solution-Focused, Goal-Setting Language for Specific Problems

Issue	Acknowledging	Clarifying	Goal Setting
	Reflect in the past tense, reflect global as partial, and reflect truth claims as perceptions; match language and position	*Define in specific behavioral terms the circumstance, exceptions, and solution attempts*	*Restate as the presence of something; specific, small, positive, and meaningful steps*
Abuse and Trauma	Sounds like you managed to get through some very difficult experiences that lots of other people would not have been able to handle. I'm impressed with you for seeking some help with a tough time.	What have you done to manage so well so far? Tell me about the times when you feel like your old self even for a short time. What was going on? What was different about you? Who else noticed?	What will it look like when you have gotten back to your old self? What difference will it make to feel like you again? What will be the first small sign that it is happening?
Academic Failure (homework, study skills)	You've had some trouble with getting homework done and studying for tests in the past.	Sounds like you haven't passed everything yet. Tell me about the times when you are able to get your work done. What are you doing at those times?	So, when you are on the path to getting better grades, what will you be doing that will show that? What else will happen when you are able to get your homework done and improve your study skills?
Anger (violence, fighting)	So, fighting has been a pretty frequent occurrence for you in the past? What would you rather do than fight?	What's been going on when you _____ instead of letting fighting take over? Tell me like I'm looking at a videotape—what happens? How did you do that?	Hey, that's really smart! How did you come up with that idea? What difference will it make when you are able to do that all of the time instead of fighting? Sounds like you want that for yourself!
Anxiety	Being worried about stuff has been on your mind a lot. How have you coped with that? What have you done to keep it from being worse?	What will you be doing differently that will show you are more mellow? If you were not worrying, what would you be doing instead or differently?	When you are in control of anxiety, what difference will that make for you? What will be the first small sign that you are calmly taking care of business?

(continues)

Interviewing for Solutions-Focused, Goal-Setting Language for Specific Problems

SOS! A Practical Guide

Issue	Acknowledging	Clarifying	Goal Setting
Attention (poor concentration, impulsivity)	Sounds like your trouble with attention has caused lots of problems in school and with friends.	From what you say, there are times when attention is not such a problem—what's happening then? What is different for you? How have you been able to do that?	When you concentrate, what will you be doing that will show you that you can pay attention?
Behavior Problems (disruptive, lying, cheating, stealing)	Sounds like the bad stuff you have been involved in has caused you problems. How would you rather things be?	Tell me about some times when you could have _____ but didn't. What was going on then? What difference did it make for you? Who else noticed? How did they let you know they noticed?	What will _____ (referral source) say you will be doing that will tell her you don't need to come to counseling anymore?
Depression	You have really felt some sadness lately.	Tell me about the times in your life when you have felt a little less sad or even a little happy. What's different for you then?	When you are happier, what will you be doing that will tell you that you are happier? So, you're thinking that what you'd like is to get some relief from the sadness? What will be the first small sign that you do have some happiness?
Divorce	From what you're saying, it sounds like you have been having a rough time with the changes in your family. I'm impressed with your ability to cope. How have you been able to do that?	Tell me about your family and the good things that you are reminded of with each person. What about your relationships with your family members would you like to see continue? What difference will it make in your life?	So, you'd like to continue to be close to your father. What difference will that make to you when that happens? What would I see you doing when you are close? Sounds like we're working toward seeing you doing that much of the time.
Drugs and Alcohol	You've really gotten the sense that you have been having some serious problems with using drugs.	What difference will it make in your life when you can avoid using drugs? Tell me about a time when you would have used drugs but didn't for some reason. What was going on? How were you able to do that?	What will you be doing instead of using drugs? What difference will that make for you? What will be the first small sign that you are achieving this goal? What will _____ (referral source) notice that will tell her you are staying sober?
Eating Disorders	Eating has been an issue of concern to you for some time now. How would you like things to be?	Tell me about a time when your family wasn't making an issue of your eating, if even for a little bit. How did you do that? Have you already done some things that let you know you are heading in the right direction?	When you envision a future in which your problems are solved, what is different for you? What are you doing differently? What is the first sign that will tell you that your problem is no longer there? What will you be doing instead?
Family Conflict	Sounds like your family has been dealing with a lot lately.	Tell me about the times when your parents didn't interfere with the choices you made, even a little bit. What did that do for you? When you think of the time when things were a little more comfortable for you, what was happening? What will your parents say they appreciated about you at that time?	So, when you reach your goal of becoming more comfortable talking to them about your ideas and feelings, what difference will it make for you? What will you be doing that's different from what you're doing now?"

(continues

Issue	Acknowledging	Clarifying	Goal Setting
Grief and Loss	You have really missed _____ in your life. If you looked through _____'s eyes for a minute, what would you see in yourself that you could appreciate? What do you think might happen if you began to appreciate this in yourself right now?	What is it about that relationship that you want to continue? What was good about your life with _____ that you want to keep going?	When you are continuing that, how will others know? What will _____ (referral source) notice that tells her you are doing that?
Opposition	Sometimes you have messed with people and have been fighting.	Is that something you want to stop doing? So, if you were to stop messing with people sometimes, what will you be doing instead? Tell me about the times when you're temped to mess with people but you do something else.	What will you say you need to do differently? Is that something that you want to work on? What difference will it make in your life when you are able to do that? What will be the first small sign that you are beginning to do that?
Relationship problems (friends, intimacy)	You've been having a rough time with your friend(s) lately.	When you're being friendly, what will you be doing that will show that? Tell me about the times when things are going better with your friends, if even just a little bit. What's happening then? What are the things that you would like to see continue?	Suppose a miracle has occurred and your problem with your friends is solved. What will be the first thing you notice about yourself that will tell you the problem is solved? What difference will it make in your life?
Reluctant or Mandated	What do you think would need to happen so that _____ was off your back?	When have those things happened a little already? What was going on then? What did you do to make those times happen?	Well, what do you think? By being here and meeting with me, will _____ be your ultimate goal? What will tell you that you have really achieved that?"
Suicide (gestures, threats, and attempts)	Sounds like things have really been tough. With all this going on, I am amazed at your ability to cope.	Tell me, how have you kept from hurting yourself over the past few months and stayed alive in spite of all you're dealing with? What else helped you stay alive? Have there been times during the past few months when things were really hard and you found a small way out just for a little while?	Sounds like your goal of using various resources to set aside your feelings works for you. What will you be doing differently when you are able to that? How will others know that you are doing that? What difference will it make in your life when you are doing that?
Test Anxiety	You have gotten pretty anxious lately when faced with a big test.	Tell me about a time when you managed to control your anxiety, even for a little bit. What were you doing differently? How did you know how to do that? What did _____ (referral source) notice about how you did that?	What do you want to accomplish in counseling? What do you think is the most important thing we need to change about this situation? What will be the first small sign to you that things are getting better?
Truancy	Sounds like you haven't passed your classes lately and have felt like giving up. I'm impressed that you're here today with all of that going on. How is that you have been able to get yourself up and get to school on the days you have come?	So, are you saying that if you were trying harder and were doing better in school, you would be more satisfied and attend school more frequently?	What will it look like when you are trying harder and are doing better in school? What difference will it make in your life? What will be the first thing you notice that will tell you it is happening?

Solution-Focused Interview Guide

Student: _____ Date: _____

Step	Sample Language	Notes
Student's Goal Find out what needs to happen (student's goal) in order for treatment to be useful for the student.	"What would you say needs to happen here (in our time together) that would make you feel it had been worthwhile? How do you want things to be?"	
Verify Understanding Verify that the counselor's understanding of the goal is accurate by asking difference questions or scaling questions. If the goal in unclear, repeat first step.	"What difference will it make when _____ happens? Who else will notice? What difference will that make? On a scale of 1 to 10, with 1 being the not at all and 10 being completely achieved, where are you now in the achievement of this goal?"	1 2 3 4 5 6 7 8 9 10
Miracle Question Ask the miracle questions and get as many details about the miracle as possible.	"Suppose tonight while you are asleep a miracle happens and this problem is completely solved. What will be the first thing you notice when you wake up that will tell you the miracle has happened? What difference will that make for you? Who else will notice? What difference will that make for you?"	
Exceptions Listen for exceptions and follow up on them by getting as many details as possible. If no exceptions are identified, go to the next step.	"When does this miracle happen even a little bit? What are you doing to make that happen? How are you managing to keep things from being worse? When are you able to beat the problem, even a little?"	
Scaling Ask a scaling question to determine the student's current level(s) of progress toward goals.	"So, on a scale of 1 to 10 (10 is that your miracle has come true and 1 is that your problem is the worst it has been), where are you right now? What lets you know that it is a _____ and not a _____ (lower number)?"	1 2 3 4 5 6 7 8 9 10

(continues)

Solution-Focused Interview Guide

Step	Sample Language	Notes
Successful Efforts Referring to the previous scaling question, find out what the student has done to reach and maintain the current level of progress.	"Wow! That number is pretty high. How have you been able to do that? Even though it's been tough, you've been able to do that?" (Reinforce successful efforts to show it was not just "luck.")	
Others' Scale Find out where on the previously mentioned scale the kids think others in their lives would rate them.	"Where would your mother (father, coach, teacher, assistant principal) say you are on this scale of 1 to 10? What will (the referral source) be seeing when you are at a 10? What difference will it make when (the referral source) is able to see that? What difference will that make?"	1 2 3 4 5 6 7 8 9 10
Others' Description Find out what kids think the significant people would say that they are doing that caused them to rate the kid at the level described in the previous step.	"If (referral source) was here, what do you think she would tell me she currently sees in you that would make her rate you a _____ rather than a _____ (lower number)?"	
Difference Ask the kids what difference they think significant others would say the behaviors identified are making.	"What difference would you say those behaviors are having? What else does it tell her to see you hanging in there?"	
Goal Scaling Ask the kids where on the scale they hope to be by the next session. Continue to ask questions about how they will know they are at this specific place on the scale, what will be different then, etc.	"Where on the scale of 1 to 10 do you hope to be by the next time we get together? How will you know you are a _____? Suppose you are at a _____ (higher number). What do you think would have happened for you to be there? What will be different when you are there? Who else will notice? What difference will that make?"	1 2 3 4 5 6 7 8 9 10
Confidence Scaling If kids rate themselves high on the scale, use scaling questions for them to rate their confidence in their ability to sustain changes (or to scale the referral source's confidence that the students can sustain the changes).	"On a scale of 1 to 10, with 10 as complete confidence that you can maintain the changes you have made, and 1 as no confidence at all, where would you put yourself?"	1 2 3 4 5 6 7 8 9 10
Task Development Based on responses to questions, invite the kid to assign homework to himself or herself.	"I'm wondering what is the most important thing you did before coming here today that helped you to get to that point on the scale? If this was next week and you were telling me how you reached number _____ on the scale, what would you tell me you did to stay so focused?"	

Note. From *Solution-Focused Brief Therapy* (pp. 30–42), by T. Pichot and Y. M. Dolan, 2003, Binghampton, NY: The Haworth Clinical Practice Press. Copyright by The Haworth Clinical Practice Press. Adapted with permission.

6 Facilitating Group Sessions

SOS Group Format

The previous chapters have described the components of the SOS group work model. In this chapter we put the components to work in a six-session unit to show how the model works. In practice, each group session uses the solution-focused dialogue and the group setting as the structure and combines dialogue and setting with brief psychoeducational lessons to teach group members skills that can be readily used to further their goals.

SOS Group Format

The SOS group process has three key ingredients: a supportive group environment, the solution-focused approach, and social–emotional skills content. The process is so versatile that it can be used to address any student issue with any age group. The variety of presenting problems addressed in a single SOS group is illustrated in the following example of Mrs. Barnes's group.

 ### A MIDDLE SCHOOL GROUP BEGINS

The counselor, Mrs. Barnes, is preparing to lead a group of sixth graders. She accepted referrals to the group from teachers, students, and parents. Of the six students she decided to include, two were referred because of social adjustment problems in the classroom; one student's parents had recently divorced; two were referred for explosive anger; and one wanted to learn how to stop procrastinating. When she met individually with each student she was able to acknowledge their perceptions of their problems, help them to articulate specific goals, and begin the process of looking for exceptions and thinking about solutions. Mrs. Barnes described how SOS groups worked and made a contract with each student. These students (all of whom had very different concerns) left their individual interviews with established goals and the sense of a process that would address their concerns.

As you read the following sections, imagine yourself in Mrs. Barnes's place with students from your own SOS group. Because you have met with each student individually before the group begins, students already will have defined their goals and have some idea of how group members help one another to reach goals. Because presenting problems can vary greatly, there is a predictable format for each six-session unit and each individual SOS group meeting.

First Meeting

The first meeting establishes the culture of the group and models the process that will be followed. This meeting sets the tone for subsequent meetings, and students will leave with the sense of whether or not the group will be a safe, helpful place to work on their goals.

If you have not previously established group agreements, then with the group's input develop a list of agreements. (See Chapter 5 for details on establishing group agreements.) Be specific as you discuss what confidentiality is, and why it is important to maintain it among group members. Emphasize the importance of being on time. Stress that each member's voice is important. The goal is for students to understand that the group is a place to come and talk about their concerns, learn problem-solving techniques and other new skills, and leave with a plan to achieve their goals.

Take time in the first meeting to have the students restate their goals for the group. You will have the members' goals that were written down and placed in their goal folders at the initial interviews. Do not be surprised that a goal that seemed crystal clear in the initial interview is not clear at all when the group meets. Take the time to be sure that students articulate their goals. Remember that the students' goals should reflect the presence rather than the absence of something. When students speak of the problem, try reflecting in a way that states their concerns as preferred goals rather than as problems to be gotten rid of (O'Hanlon & Beadle, 1997). With clear goals, group members can do their solution-focused work. We suggest that you make use of scaling questions to set the stage for focus on definable progress. (See Chapter 5 for a review of the characteristics of effective goals and use of scaling.)

The psychoeducational activity in the first group session can be an introductions activity. Students at every age seem to enjoy sharing their own characteristics and usually end up learning some things about themselves as well as others.

Subsequent Meetings

Subsequent meetings resemble the first meeting, with a regular check-in that includes stating goals and scaling. An important leadership task is to encourage members to help one another with progress toward solutions. Goal folders provide an easy review of member progress. Each session includes a skill development activity that is content and level specific. (See Chapter 8 for activities and lesson plans.)

Following the activity, use bridging statements or questions from the skills content to help students reflect on how these new skills will help them work on their goals over the next week (or the time period between group sessions). Plan for the next meeting, and end the session with evaluation. Evaluation is a regular part of SOS group meetings as leaders ask the members to assess how the group is working for them. Finally, the group leader evaluates each meeting on the group session plan.

Group Graduation

In schools, we like to think of group closure as graduation rather than termination. This is another way we signify the growth in skills and knowledge gained through the SOS group experience. Some students will achieve the completion of their goals, and others will continue to work on them after the group ends. Note that, according to Murphy (1997), complete resolution of the problem is not required for termination. Whether you plan to implement a six-session unit or multiple six-session units, prepare to help the members finish up their business at the final session. Graduation is a really effective way to highlight each student's growth and "blame" them for their successes. Since you and the students establish specific goals in the beginning, you and the students will be in a good position to compliment all members on their successes. The following is an example of one middle school counselor's closing comments.

 WRAPPING UP THE GROUP

The counselor wanted to have group graduation for a group of eighth graders who had been working together for six sessions. She wanted to compliment them and remind them of the goals they had identified. She said, "I'm really impressed with the changes you've made, and it seems to me that you all have a good sense of what you need to do to continue such changes." Then she asked the students to share with one another the improvements they had seen and expected to continue to see in one another. She concluded by saying, "With these changes you've made, and with your plans to keep doing what's working for you, I'm comfortable with completing our time as a group. I would like to have us touch bases with one another in a booster session in about a month to check up on things. How does that sound?"

This counselor focused on the gains toward goals and in skill development to help facilitate the group's closure. Using their goals as guidelines, she asked the students to reflect on what they were doing successfully and how they were able to do that. Students were asked to share with others their plans for continued improvement and how they could face any setbacks that occurred. In addition to the planned booster session, you can, of course, leave the door open for future visits to check on progress.

Summary

- The approaches of solution-focused counseling, combined with the skill development of psychoeducational groups, help students identify and work toward the achievement of their own goals while learning specific skills to better reach their goals.

- From the first meeting through graduation, the SOS group process has a structure that is focused and predictable for the leader and the members.

- The SOS group leader teaches the solution-focused process and encourages group members to use it for themselves and to help one another.

- The SOS format is a six-session unit that can be used as a single course of six sessions or can be repeated for multiple units to accommodate longer-term groups.

- Booster sessions are useful, planned support for members of SOS groups following graduation.

Part 2

SOS Groups:
The Content

7 Six-Session Group Unit

The group session outlines that follow provide an at-a-glance version of the structure for a six-session SOS unit. Words in italics are suggested language to use with students. Refer to Chapter 3 to review group interventions and Chapter 5 for a review of solution-focused approaches. As you go through the sessions remember that you will be using the solution-focused approach with the group, teaching members to use the approach to help themselves and one another, and encouraging member interaction. It is essential to keep in mind the maturity level of the group in your expectations and your choice of language.

Materials You Will Need for the Six-Session Unit
- Group roll sheet*
- Name tags
- Group agreement chart*
- Goal folder for each member*
- Group notes and evaluation forms* (6)
- Six group activities, one per content area, with accompanying materials (see Chapter 8 for activities and lesson plans)

*Materials available in Chapter 8 and as reproducible forms on the *Resources* CD

Session I

I. Call Roll

   Have group members make name tags.

II. Group Introduction

   Welcome to the group! This is our time together in a place to come and talk about concerns. We're going to learn how you've solved problems in the past, learn some new skills, and come up with your plan for working on your goals.

III. Group Agreement

You may choose to post your selected group agreements on the group room wall. *We need to have a few understandings so that our group will be a good experience for everyone. Let's talk about them for a moment.* [Discuss the agreements.] *How will these agreements help us as a group?*

You may direct your question to one member or look to the group as a whole. After one member has answered, compliment the effort and look to other members to extend and amplify the interaction.

IV. Activity for Session I

Select an activity from the Self-Knowledge and Acceptance skills content area to use with the group.

V. Individual Problems Discussion

Ask each member to talk briefly about what he or she wants to achieve by being in the group.

We're interested in all of you. Could you each tell us briefly what you would like to achieve in our group? How will you know when things are better for you?

As members tell their stories watch for opportunities to "connect the dots" or "disconnect the dots" between members to encourage group cohesion. Also, watch for opportunities to connect the skills content in the activity to individual members' goals.

VI. Goal Folders

Distribute group goal folders and describe how the folders will be used at check-in at the beginning of each session.

This is your goal folder. We'll work on it each time we have group. In each folder we've written the goal that you set for yourself. At the beginning of each meeting we will check in with one another about the progress we've made toward our goals.

VII. The Miracle Question

Depending on the size of the group, characteristics of members, and available time, you may choose to ask the Miracle question. Even if you do not ask the Miracle question, remind them of it. At this point the task is for members to restate their goals. The question can be used simply as an introduction to restating goals or, if time allows, it can be a vehicle for developing group cohesion.

Many of you have answered this question at our first individual meeting, but the other group members did not hear your answer. It's important for the other members to hear what you have to say. If you each woke up tomorrow and discovered that a miracle had occurred overnight, what would be different as you went through your day that would tell you a miracle had occurred?

If you do ask the question, select follow-up questions that fit each member's situation.

What will be the first sign that this occurred?

What will you being doing differently?

Who will be the first to notice the difference in you?

What will that person notice?

How will that person respond to you when he or she observes this difference?

How will you respond to him or her in return?

Involve other group members in the process of getting additional details in response to the follow-up questions. After asking several detail questions, ask other members to ask questions to get the details. This will encourage interaction and help teach the solution-focused process.

VIII. Difference

Ask students to talk to one another about the effect of the miracle on their lives. Use the following kinds of questions to encourage interaction.

What difference will it make for you when you are able to _____?

What would _____ say when they notice you managing _____?

Suppose I was viewing a videotape of you with this problem much improved. What would I see you doing?

Some day when the problem that brought you here today doesn't bother you as much, what will you get to do more?

IX. Exceptions

Ask members to reflect upon times when the problem has been not so bad or has been even a little bit better.

Tell us if this miracle has already happened, even just a little bit.

When in the past has the problem not interfered?

X. Compliment

Identify things the members have already been doing to make the situation better.

What have you been doing already to make things better? Wow! How were you able to do that? How have you kept things from getting worse?

XI. Scaling

Discuss how scaling will be used each session. Ask the members to scale the current level of achievement of their goals.

Here's how it works. The scale of 1 to 10 shows that 1 is when things are the worst they can be and 10 is the day after the miracle.

Where are you right now?

Wow! How do you do that?

Ask members to note on the scaling form what number they would give themselves today.

XII. Task Development

Develop tasks that are nonspecific and convey that members are trusted to complete the homework in ways that work best for them.

Let's talk now about what you might do in this next week that will assist you in keeping the problem at a distance in your life, so you can do what you really want to do.

What will you do this week to raise your rating?

What's been working that you can try again?

What can you see yourself doing differently to move from a #_____ to a #_____?

XIII. Ongoing Evaluation by Group Members

We ask group members to give us feedback on how the group is working for them. The following are examples of questions to request feedback:

When has group worked well? When has it worked better? What were we doing to make that happen? How would you like the group to be? What will you be doing differently when the group is working the way it would be most helpful to you?

XIV. Dismiss the Group

XV. Complete Group Notes and Evaluation

Sessions II through V

I. Check Roll and Distribute Goal Folders

II. Status Check-In

Choose questions that fit:

What's better this week?

What went well for you this week in relation to your goal?

Describe the things you noticed that were better about what you're working on this week.

Throughout each meeting watch for opportunities to encourage group members to be helpful to one another.

III. Scale Progress

Ask the group:

On a scale of 1 to 10, where are you with your goal?

Ask members what number they would give themselves today. Have them note the number in their goals folder.

IV. Compliment

If the situation is better, stress the effects of the student's behaviors on others and reinforce what the student did to make it happen:

Wow! What does a #_____ look like? What did you do to make it better?

If the situation is the same, elicit the details, amplify, and reinforce what the student did to make it happen or keep things from getting worse:

How did you manage to keep things from getting worse? (Listen for what is better.)

If nothing is better or it's worse, acknowledge and question for exceptions:

Man, that's tough. Was there a time when it was a little better, say a #_____?

What will improvement look like?

How will you know when things are better for you?

V. Difference

What difference did it make for you that you were at a #_____?

What would _____ say she or he noticed about you when you are at a #_____?

Suppose I was viewing a videotape of you with this problem much improved. What would I see you doing?

Some day when the problem that brought you here today doesn't bother you as much, what will you get to do more?

VI. Exceptions

When in the past has the problem not interfered?

How were you able to do that?

VII. Activity for Session II: Select from the Interpersonal and Communication Skills content area

Activity for Session III: Select from the Responsible Behavior content area

Activity for Session IV: Select from the Conflict Resolution content area

Activity for Session V: Select from the Decision-Making content area

VIII. Apply Lesson to Goals

What difference will it make for you that you are able to use these skills with others?

IX. Task Development

Let's talk now about what you might do in this next week that will assist you in keeping the problem at a distance in your life, so you can do what you really want to do.

What will you do this week to raise your rating?

What's been working that you could do more of?

What can you see yourself doing differently to move from a #_____ to a #_____?

X. Evaluation by Group Members

Ask about how group is working for everyone.

What's working well for you in group? What would you like to be different?

XI. Dismiss the Group

If this group is ending, remind members that the next session will be the last. Give a homework assignment. Ask members to write things that they will remember about their group experience.

XII. Complete Group Notes and Evaluation

Session VI

I. Check Roll

Distribute goal folders. Remind students that this is the last session and invite them to share thoughts and feelings about unfinished business and the ending of the group. If the group is continuing, this session will follow the format of Sessions II through V.

II. Status Check-In

What's better this week?

What went well for you this week in relation to your goal?

Describe the things you noticed that were better about what you're working on this week.

III. Scale Progress

IV. Compliment

If the situation is better, amplify the effects of the student's behaviors on others and reinforce what the student did to make it happen:

Wow! What does a #_____ look like? What did you do to make it better?

If the situation is the same, elicit the details, amplify, and reinforce what the student did to make it happen or keep things from getting worse:

How did you manage to keep things from getting worse? (Listen for what is better.)

If nothing is better or it's worse, acknowledge and listen for what is better:

Man, that's tough. Was there a time when it was a little better, say a #_____?

What will improvement look like?

How will you know when things are better for you?

V. Difference

Help group members to ask these questions of one another by modeling and asking:

What difference did it make for you that you were at a #_____?

What would _____ say he or she noticed about you when you are at a #_____?

Suppose I was viewing a videotape of you with this problem much improved. What would I see you doing?

Some day when the problem that brought you here today doesn't bother you as much, what will you get to do more?

VI. Exceptions

When in the past has the problem not interfered?

How were you able to do that?

VII. Activity

Select an activity from the Self-Care and Self-Management content area

VIII. Apply Lesson to Goals

How will remembering the things you have done so well help you if you encounter difficulties?

IX. Celebrate Successes

Talk about the attitudes and behaviors that were present when the group began, the topics that were discussed, the homework assignments, the progress made with respect to their goals, and what still needs to be accomplished.

I'm really impressed with the changes you've made. It seems to me that you each have a good sense of what you need to do to continue such changes.

X. Graduation

Ask the students to share with others their plans for continued improvement and how they will face any setbacks that occur. Of course, you can leave the door open for future visits to check on progress. If you plan to have a bonus or booster session at a later date, this is the time to let the group members know.

Let's think back to the goals that each of you set for yourself at the beginning of the group. Think of the progress you have made. We learned some skills for using I-Messages, confronting others appropriately, choosing anger styles that work, making decisions, and taking care of ourselves. Please tell the group how you plan to continue to make progress toward your goal even when some challenges come along.

Help group members solicit improvements and give compliments to others:

Share, if you will, the improvements you have noticed in others in the group. _____(name), please ask _____(name) how he/she has been able to improve things.

XI. Dismiss the Group

XII. Complete Group Notes and Evaluation

Booster Sessions

An additional session or two can be scheduled from a few weeks to a month following the end of group. Booster or bonus sessions provide a built-in follow-up that allows you and group members to check in on continued progress. The skills learned in the group and the solution-focused process can be reinforced again after students have had a short period of time to work toward their goals. Some ideas for discussion questions are:

- *Since we were last together, what have you noticed in your life (family, relationship, at school, etc.) that you want to continue to happen?*

- *What have you done to make that happen? How were you able to do that?*

Select an activity that the kids enjoyed during group sessions and reinforce the skills taught with additional opportunities for practice. Kids always seem to enjoy and benefit from activities that provide lots of scenarios for practice of the skills they have learned. Ask the students if you may call on them in the future for their ideas and suggestions for helping others deal with situations similar to those that they have successfully changed. Some counselors call this the "Consultant Club," which is composed of former members and others who have demonstrated expertise in overcoming school problems. Finally, offering students an open door for future contacts seems to reduce any apprehension surrounding the ending of group.

Summary

- Use the solution-focused approach with the group and teach members to use it to help themselves and one another.

- Session I is unique because this is the time to establish the group agreements and the process that includes solution-focused dialogue about goals and the opportunity to develop skills.

- Sessions II through V continue the solution-focused dialogue with and between group members and include instruction for skills in the areas of Interpersonal and Communication Skills, Responsible Behavior, Conflict Resolution, Decision Making, and Self-Care.

- Session VI wraps up the group, so be sure to include some graduation rituals for group members.

- Booster sessions can be used for follow-up and reinforcement after the group has ended to ease the transition and support behavior change.

8 SOS Group Lesson Plans and Activities

This chapter includes the lesson plans, activities, and reproducible materials for the psychoeducational portion of each SOS group session. The lessons are organized in the following content areas:

- Self-Knowledge and Acceptance
- Interpersonal and Communication Skills
- Responsible Behavior and Personal Responsibility
- Conflict Resolution
- Decision Making
- Self-Care and Self-Management

Each content area is organized as:

- Content Area
- Level
- Lesson (one for each unit)

For example, the Self-Knowledge and Acceptance section is organized as follows:

Self-Knowledge and Acceptance	Primary	Unit I
		Unit II
		Unit III
	Intermediate	Unit I
		Unit II
		Unit III
	Secondary	Unit I
		Unit II
		Unit III

Each content area includes three group sessions for each level (Primary, Intermediate, and Secondary), for a total of fifty-four lessons. Activities and reproducible sheets follow each lesson plan. The CD-ROM accompanying this book includes a printable version of each reproducible student handout. See comprehensive lists of primary-, intermediate-, and secondary-level group topics with objectives and activities on pages xiii–xviii. See also Appendixes 2.A through 2.C for primary, intermediate, and secondary multiple-unit group schedules.

Lesson plans include objectives, materials, procedure, discussion, and evaluation. Leader notes are added where appropriate to provide relevant information. Suggested discussion starters are outlined in each lesson. Often, the greatest benefits from group experiences come from the thorough processing of discussion questions.

The lessons are designed to provide three levels of activities for the groups that meet for up to three units.

Discovery Hunt

Objectives
The group members will get to know other members and recognize that there is something unique about everyone.

Materials
Discovery Hunt sheet* for every student; pencils

Procedure
1. Introduce the activity by telling the children that they are going on a discovery hunt to find out some things about their group members.
2. Allow group members to circulate, asking "Which of these ideas is like you?"
3. Have group members write their name on the line in the box they match.
4. After an allotted time have members return to the group.

Discussion
1. "What did you learn about someone else in the group?" Share examples.
2. "Could everyone's name go into every square of the sheet? Why or why not?"
3. "What does this activity tell us about the members of this group?"
4. "What is good about people being different from each other?"
5. "How are you like or different from someone else in the group?"
6. "How do you feel about being similar or different from others?"

Evaluation
Group members identify at least one valuable, unique characteristic of another group member and themselves.

Leader Note
The important point to emphasize in the discussion is that everyone is unique and that although there are many ways in which we are like other people, there are also ways in which we are different. Help children understand that being different doesn't make one better or worse—just unique.

115

---

* Also available on CD

Note. From *Thinking, Feeling, Behaving: Grades 1–6* (p. 11), by A. Vernon, 1989, Champaign, IL: Research Press. Copyright 1989 by Research Press. Adapted with permission.

Discovery Hunt

Name _____

One at a time, go to each person in your group. Ask "Which of these ideas is like you?" Each person should write his or her first name on the line.

116

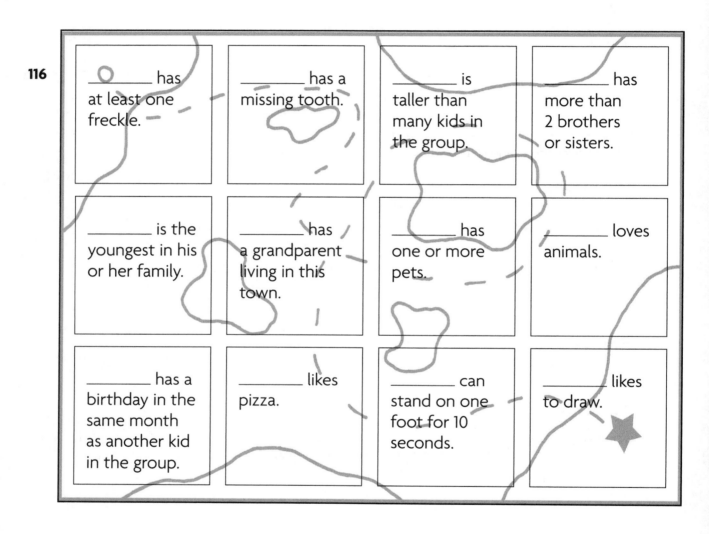

_____ has at least one freckle.

_____ has a missing tooth.

_____ is taller than many kids in the group.

_____ has more than 2 brothers or sisters.

_____ is the youngest in his or her family.

_____ has a grandparent living in this town.

_____ has one or more pets.

_____ loves animals.

_____ has a birthday in the same month as another kid in the group.

_____ likes pizza.

_____ can stand on one foot for 10 seconds.

_____ likes to draw.

Note. From *Thinking, Feeling, Behaving: Grades 1–6* (p. 12), by A. Vernon, 1989, Champaign, IL: Research Press. Copyright 1989 by Research Press. Adapted with permission.

Identify Your Feelings

Objectives

The group members will be able to identify their own feelings as they occur.

Materials

10 situation cards: *Identify Your Feelings**

Procedure

1. Discuss the feelings that occur on an everyday basis. Describe how you know when you are scared, happy, sad, and so forth.

2. Discuss blushing, tightening of stomach, perspiring, and nervousness as physical sensations connected to feelings.

3. Use situation cards to have group members tell (a) how they would feel, (b) what clue their body gives them, and (c) how they could express the feeling.

117

Discussion

1. "What are some ways we can express feelings appropriately?"

2. "How does it help to pay attention to the clues our bodies give us about our feelings?"

Evaluation

Have each group member respond to the following situations and observe appropriate expression of feelings.

1. "You are frustrated with a school assignment. How does your body feel? What can you do?"

2. "Your parents forgot to do something with you that they promised they'd do. How do you feel?"

Leader Note

Feelings are a part of your personality. Identifying feelings is the first step to dealing with and expressing feelings. Discuss with your students why we need to identify feelings. Some students may fear this skill because they don't want to show their feelings.

---

* Also available on CD

Note. From *Getting to Know You! Social Skills Curriculum for Grades 1–3* (p. 105), by D. Hanken and J. Kennedy, 1998, Minneapolis, MN: Educational Media Corporation. Copyright 1998 by Educational Media Corporation. Adapted with permission.

Identify Your Feelings

118

You lost a tooth SKA-P-2	You learned to read SKA-P-2
Your friend hit you SKA-P-2	You lost a book SKA-P-2
Your parents punished you for lying SKA-P-2	You moved to a new school SKA-P-2
Your grandparents came from out of town to visit SKA-P-2	You lost your jacket SKA-P-2
You had to stay in for recess SKA-P-2	You made a new friend SKA-P-2

Note. From *Getting to Know You! Social Skills Curriculum for Grades 1–3* (p. 105), by D. Hanken and J. Kennedy, 1998, Minneapolis, MN: Educational Media Corporation. Copyright 1998 by Educational Media Corporation. Adapted with permission.

Showing Your Feelings

Objectives
Group members will identify feelings and choose how and when to express them.

Materials
Posters that show feelings; lists of feelings; *Showing Your Feelings* situation cards*

Procedure
1. Discuss physical sensations that go with different feelings.
2. Discuss how people deal with feelings: express them, exercise, walk away, talk with a friend.
3. Discuss inappropriate ways of dealing with feelings: fighting or hitting, suppressing feelings.
4. Give the group various situations and have them role-play in groups of three, with one member sharing feelings, one listening, and one giving feedback.
5. Have group members role-play the appropriate expression of feelings.

Discussion
1. "How does identifying sensations in our body associated with feelings help us?"
2. "When we can identify those sensations, how can we make decisions about how to respond to our feelings?"

Evaluation
Present an additional scenario to the group and ask members to identify their bodily sensations and the appropriate expression of feelings.

Leader Note
It is important that students learn to identify sensations in their bodies associated with feelings (butterflies in stomach, heart beating fast) and to know that healthy expression of feelings is essential for physical and mental health.

119

---

* Also available on CD

Note. From *Getting to Know You! Social Skills Curriculum for Grades 1–3* (p. 108), by D. Hanken and J. Kennedy, 1998, Minneapolis, MN: Educational Media Corporation. Copyright 1998 by Educational Media Corporation. Adapted with permission.

SOS! *A Practical Guide*

Showing Your Feelings

120

You are the last one
picked for a game.

SKA-P-3

Your brother or sister won't let you
come into his or her bedroom.

SKA-P-3

Your best friend ignores
you at recess.

SKA-P-3

It's going to snow.

SKA-P-3

There is no school tomorrow.

SKA-P-3

Your cousin is coming.

SKA-P-3

You're going shopping.

SKA-P-3

Your friend is moving.

SKA-P-3

You may move to another town.

SKA-P-3

You get picked for the team.

SKA-P-3

Note. From *Getting to Know You! Social Skills Curriculum for Grades 1–3* (p. 108), by D. Hanken and J. Kennedy, 1998, Minneapolis, MN: Educational Media Corporation. Copyright 1998 by Educational Media Corporation. Adapted with permission.

Getting to Know You

Objectives
Group members will share information about themselves̲ ̲ ̲ ̲ ̲ ̲ ̲ ̲ ̲ ̲ ̲ p
members.

Materials
Discussion cards*; *Getting to Know You and Me* sharing c̲

Procedure
1. The group leader selects one card from the stack and models a response that is brief and to the point.

2. Going around the group, each group member responds to the same prompt.

3. Each group member takes a turn drawing a card from the stack, reading it aloud, and responding. The rest of the group answers the same prompt.

4. Have at least one round per member.

121

Discussion
1. "What did you learn about the other group members that is similar to yourself?"
2. "What did you learn about yourself that you were not aware of?"

Evaluation
Observe the activity to determine that each student is able to express at least one personal description for the group.

Leader Note
Students often enjoy expressing their likes and dislikes. Prompts that encourage them to look at their values and preferences help to increase their self-awareness and build the foundation for good communication and self-advocacy.

---

* Also available on CD

I

Discussion Cards

I am best at SKA-I	Something I like about myself is SKA-I
The place I like to be most is SKA-I	I'm sure glad I SKA-I
Two things I like about myself are SKA-I	One of the best things about me is SKA-I
I'm not afraid to SKA-I	If I had a magic carpet, I'd SKA-I
I'd like to say something good about SKA-I	I'm sure glad I SKA-I

122

(continues)

Discussion Cards
(Continued)

I am unique because

SKA-I

The part of me I'd most like to change is

SKA-I

Someday

SKA-I

If I were very tiny, I would

SKA-I

My favorite part of the day is

SKA-I

I don't want to

SKA-I

If I were a giant, I'd

SKA-I

I'll never forget

SKA-I

My favorite TV show is
_____ because

SKA-I

I was really sorry I

SKA-I

Getting to Know You
and Me Sharing Cards

A Person I Admire SKA-I-1	My Favorite Place SKA-I-1
Something I Need Help With SKA-I-1	My Favorite Daydream SKA-I-1
Something I Like to Do With My Family SKA-I-1	If I Had One Wish, It Would Be SKA-I-1
Something I Really Like to Do at School SKA-I-1	One Way I Wish I Could Be Different SKA-I-1
Something I Like to Do Alone SKA-I-1	My Idea of a Perfect Saturday Afternoon SKA-I-1

(continues)

Getting to Know You
and Me Sharing Cards
(Continued)

One of the Best Things That Ever Happened to Me SKA-I-1	A Person I'd Like to Be SKA-I-1
One Thing I Am Sure I Can Do Well SKA-I-1	Something I Like to Do with Others SKA-I-1
An Important Event in My Life SKA-I-1	My Favorite Vacation SKA-I-1
The Funniest Thing That Ever Happened to Me SKA-I-1	A Friend of Mine Who Is Different From Me SKA-I-1
Something About Me That You Wouldn't Know Unless I Told You SKA-I-1	If I Could Go Anywhere in the World, I'd Go to SKA-I-1

"WANTED"

Objectives

The group members will identify their unique qualities, strengths, and special talents; share them with the group; and learn about the qualities, strengths, and special talents of other group members.

Materials

"WANTED" poster*; photos of students

Procedure

1. Remind the group that each person has unique qualities that make him or her special. Ask the group members to think about the things they are good at and really like.
2. Ask each group member to complete the WANTED poster.
3. Use photos, if available, or have students draw their self-portraits.
4. Have group members share their responses.
5. Display WANTED posters in the group room.

Discussion

1. "What did you learn about yourself that you might not have realized?"
2. "What did you learn about your group mates that you didn't know?"

Evaluation

Review students' WANTED posters for inclusion of strengths information.

Leader Note

Becoming aware of personal strengths and being able to talk about them enhance students' senses of self. Help students become aware that they do have strengths, have unique qualities, and are special.

126

---

* Also available on CD

Note. From *Esteem Builders* (p. 134), by M. Borba, 1989, Austin, TX: PRO-ED, Inc. Copyright 1989 by PRO-ED, Inc. Adapted with permission.

WANTED

You are wanted by your group mates for being special.

Age: _____

Weight: _____

Height: _____

Eye Color: _____

Hair Color: _____

Picture of Wanted Student

Most Likely to Be Found:

_____

_____

_____

Special Skills and Talents:

_____

_____

_____

Best Known for:

_____

_____

_____

Likes to:

_____

_____

_____

Note. From *Esteem Builders* (p. 134), by M. Borba, 1989, Austin, TX: PRO-ED, Inc. Copyright 1989 by PRO-ED, Inc. Adapted with permission.

How We See Ourselves:
Self-Assessment, Sharing, and Discussion

Objectives
Group members will:

1. rate the degree to which they possess specific qualities or characteristics,
2. represent their self-concept pictorially or in words, and
3. describe how self-concept affects daily living.

128

Materials
Looking at Me Self-Assessment sheet* for each student; markers

Procedure
1. Begin with a brief discussion about self-concept. Distribute the sheets and briefly review the directions. Give the students about 10 minutes to complete the sheet. Make markers available for students who wish to draw pictures of themselves instead of writing paragraphs.
2. Have members share their self-assessments and drawings or paragraphs. Emphasize that all sharing is voluntary, and that students may keep any or all parts of the sheet confidential if they choose.

Discussion
1. "What did you learn about yourself that surprised you?"
2. "What strengths did your self-assessment reveal?"
3. "What qualities would you like to develop further?"
4. "What qualities would you like to reduce or eliminate?"
5. "What qualities or concerns did you discover you have in common with other members of the group?"
6. "How does self-concept affect our performance at school? ... our relations with other people? ... our outlook on life and the future?"

Evaluation
Review students' self-assessments and drawings or paragraphs for completeness. Students should be·able to talk about how their self-concept affects them in their daily lives.

Leader Note
Remind the students that self-concept is like looking in the mirror, except that the image we have depends more on thoughts and conclusions about ourselves than it does on our eyesight. Point out that people often see themselves quite differently than others see them.

---

* Also available on CD

Note. From *Group Activities for Counselors* (pp. 28–30), by S. Elliot, 1994, Austin, TX: PRO-ED, Inc. Copyright 1994 by PRO-ED, Inc. Adapted with permission.

Looking at Me Self-Assessment

Read through the list of characteristics below. Decide how well each characteristic fits you. If you are unsure of an item, ask yourself how others see you. Circle the point on the scale that describes you best.

	Most of the Time	Sometimes	Almost Never			Most of the Time	Sometimes	Almost Never
1. Well-liked					19. A good friend			
2. Good-looking					20. Boring			
3. Intelligent					21. Tough			
4. Popular					22. Confident			
5. Athletic					23. Unhappy			
6. Appreciated					24. Creative			
7. Talented					25. A leader			
8. Happy					26. Friendly			
9. Worried					27. Helpful			
10. Relaxed					28. Responsible			
11. Caring					29. Fun			
12. Strong					30. Angry			
13. Unique					31. Honest			
14. Assertive					32. Successful			
15. Enthusiastic					33. A loner			
16. Energetic					34. Shy			
17. Tense					35. Generous			
18. Dependable								

129

On the other side of this paper, draw a picture or write a paragraph that describes your thoughts and feelings about yourself.

Note. From *Group Activities for Counselors* (p. 30), by S. Elliot, 1994, Austin, TX: PRO-ED, Inc. Copyright 1994 by PRO-ED, Inc. Adapted with permission.

SELF-KNOWLEDGE AND ACCEPTANCE

Something About Me
You Wouldn't Know Unless I Told You

Objectives
Group members will:

1. share something about themselves that is neither obvious nor generally known, and
2. describe what it feels like to disclose information about themselves.

130

Materials
Something About Me* cards

Procedure
1. Discuss the idea that everyone has unique characteristics. An introduction to this discussion might run something like this: *No one can figure out everything about us just by observing us or being around us at school. For example, unless I told you, none of you would know about* (fill in details from your experience). *There are many things in your lives that we can't see or guess at either. So today, let's enlighten one another a bit. Let's share things about ourselves that no one else in the group knows. Maybe you work as a volunteer at a hospital. Maybe you help out with young children at your church or synagogue. Perhaps you like to write poetry, paint, dance, or play video games. Think about it for a few moments and see if you can come up with something that will surprise us.*

2. Have group members draw prompts from the stack of *Something About Me* cards.

Discussion
1. "How does it feel to talk about something that was kind of a secret until now?"
2. "Why do you think we don't learn these things about each other outside of the group?"
3. "How can we avoid judging people based on the obvious and superficial?"

Evaluation
The group members will share at least one unique characteristic about themselves and reflect on ways they can avoid judging others based on outward appearances.

---

* Also available on CD

Note. From *50 Activities for Teaching Emotional Intelligence, Level II: Middle School* (p. 40), by D. Schilling and S. Palomares, 1996, Austin, TX: PRO-ED, Inc. Copyright 1996 by PRO-ED, Inc. Adapted with permission.

Something About Me
Discussion Cards

A Person I Admire SKA-S-1	A Secret Wish I Have SKA-S-1
Something I Like to Do Alone SKA-S-1	Something I Want to Keep SKA-S-1
Something I Like to Do With Others SKA-S-1	When I Felt Comfortable Just Being Me SKA-S-1
My Favorite Place SKA-S-1	Something About My Culture That I Appreciate SKA-S-1
My Idea of a Perfect Saturday Afternoon SKA-S-1	Something I Really Like to Do SKA-S-1

(continues)

-1

Something About Me
Discussion Cards
(*Continued*)

A Time I Felt Happy SKA-S-1	A Time I Was Scared and It Was Fun SKA-S-1
A Time I Helped Someone Who Was Afraid SKA-S-1	A Time I Really Controlled My Feelings SKA-S-1
Something I Hate to Do SKA-S-1	I Felt Good and Bad About the Same Thing SKA-S-1
Someone Who Respects My Feelings SKA-S-1	How I React When I Am Angry SKA-S-1
A Time I Couldn't Control My Curiosity SKA-S-1	A Time I Was Alone But Not Lonely SKA-S-1

Note. From *50 Activities for Teaching Emotional Intelligence, Level II: Middle School* (p. 40), by D. Schilling and S. Palomares, 1996, Austin, TX: PRO-ED, Inc. Copyright 1996 by PRO-ED, Inc. Adapted with permission.

How We See Ourselves

Objectives

Group members will:

1. rate the degree to which they possess specific qualities or characteristics,

2. represent their self-concept pictorially or in words, and

3. describe how self-concept affects daily living.

Materials

A copy of the *Looking at Me** handout for each member; markers; pens

133

Procedure

1. Begin with a brief discussion about self-concept. Remind students that self-concept is like looking in the mirror, except that the image we have depends more on our thoughts and our conclusions about ourselves than it does on eyesight. Point out that people can see themselves quite differently than others see them.

2. Distribute the *Looking at Me Self-Assessment* sheets and briefly review the directions. Make markers available for those who wish to draw pictures instead of writing paragraphs. Emphasize that all sharing is voluntary and that students may keep any part of their responses confidential if they wish.

Discussion

1. "Did you learn anything about yourself from this activity that surprised you? What was it?"

2. "What strengths did your self-assessment reveal?"

3. "What qualities would you like to develop further?"

4. "What qualities would you like to reduce or eliminate?"

5. "What qualities or concerns did you discover you have in common with other members of the group?"

6. "How does self-concept affect our performance at school? ... our relations with other people? ... our outlook on life and the future?"

Evaluation

Group members will complete the self-assessment and be able to discuss the impact of self-concept on their school experience.

* Also available on CD

Note. From *50 Activities for Teaching Emotional Intelligence, Level III: High School* (p. 74), by D. Schilling and S. Palomares, 1999, Austin, TX: PRO-ED, Inc. Copyright 1999 by PRO-ED, Inc. Adapted with permission.

⬥-2 **Looking at Me Self-Assessment**

Read through the list of characteristics below. Decide how well each characteristic fits you. If you are unsure of an item, ask yourself how others see you. Circle the point on the scale that describes you best.

134

	Most of the Time	Sometimes	Almost Never
1. Well-liked			
2. Good-looking			
3. Intelligent			
4. Popular			
5. Athletic			
6. Appreciated			
7. Talented			
8. Happy			
9. Worried			
10. Relaxed			
11. Caring			
12. Strong			
13. Unique			
14. Assertive			
15. Enthusiastic			
16. Energetic			
17. Tense			
18. Dependable			

	Most of the Time	Sometimes	Almost Never
19. A good friend			
20. Boring			
21. Tough			
22. Confident			
23. Unhappy			
24. Creative			
25. A leader			
26. Friendly			
27. Helpful			
28. Responsible			
29. Fun			
30. Angry			
31. Honest			
32. Successful			
33. A loner			
34. Shy			
35. Generous			

On the other side of this paper, draw a picture or write a paragraph that describes your thoughts and feelings about yourself.

Note. From *50 Activities for Teaching Emotional Intelligence, Level III: High School* (p. 75), by D. Schilling and S. Palomares, 1999, Austin, TX: PRO-ED, Inc. Copyright 1999 by PRO-ED, Inc. Adapted with permission.

Who Am I?

Objectives

Group members will:

1. identify likes and dislikes and areas of strength and weakness,

2. clarify personal values, and

3. explain how self-awareness facilitates performance.

Materials

A copy of the *Who Am I?* handout* for each member

135

Procedure

Distribute the *Who Am I?* experience sheets and have the group members answer the questions. When they have finished, facilitate a group discussion.

Discussion

1. "What have you learned about your strengths and weaknesses from this activity?"

2. "What have you learned about your likes and dislikes?"

3. "What insights did you gain concerning your values?"

4. "How does knowing these kinds of things about yourself help you in school and in life?"

Evaluation

Group members will complete the self-assessment and be able to discuss the impact of self-concept on their school experience.

---

* Also available on CD

Note. From *50 Activities for Teaching Emotional Intelligence, Level II: Middle School* (pp. 34–35), by D. Schilling and S. Palomares, 1996, Austin, TX: PRO-ED, Inc. Copyright 1996 by PRO-ED, Inc. Adapted with permission.

S-3

Who Am I?

An important element of successful living is knowing who you are. In order to have life goals that are meaningful, realistic, and achievable, you need an accurate sense of self-understanding. You need to know your strengths and limitations, likes and dislikes, wants and needs, and beliefs and values. The following questions will help you clarify these things.

1. What are some things you've learned quickly and easily?

_____

136

2. What is something that you learned because you kept working at it, even though it was hard?

_____

3. What are some things you've been able to show other people how to do?

_____

4. What are your talents (strengths, abilities)?

_____

5. What are some of your accomplishments?

_____

6. In what school subject or activity are you most successful?

_____

What about weaknesses? First of all, everybody's got them. You aren't alone. Here are some things that other kids have trouble with. Put a check in the box beside any of these items that apply to you.

- ☐ Using my time well
- ☐ Standing up for myself when I know I am right
- ☐ Overcoming shyness
- ☐ Building self-confidence
- ☐ Giving myself credit for achievements
- ☐ Giving myself credit for strengths
- ☐ Learning from my mistakes
- ☐ Acknowledging my present weaknesses
- ☐ Starting a conversation with a member of the opposite sex

(continues)

Examine yourself closely, and complete as many of the following items as you can.
My personal strengths (talents, accomplishments, favorite activities, etc.):

1. _____

2. _____

3. _____

4. _____

5. _____

My personal weaknesses (difficulties, limitations, things I don't know how to do yet, etc.):

1. _____

2. _____

3. _____

Admirable qualities: List the ten qualities (such as honesty, bravery, helpfulness) you most admire in people.

1. _____   6. _____

2. _____   7. _____

3. _____   8. _____

4. _____   9. _____

5. _____   10. _____

Note. From *50 Activities for Teaching Emotional Intelligence, Level II: Middle School* (pp. 35–36), by D. Schilling and S. Palomares, 1996, Austin, TX: PRO-ED, Inc. Copyright 1996 by PRO-ED, Inc. Adapted with permission.

Formulating I—Statements

Objectives
The group members will:

1. practice effective expression of their thoughts, feelings, and wants, and
2. compare the use of I—statements to less effective forms of confrontation.

Materials
*Getting Your Message Across** experience sheet for each student; chalkboard and chalk

Procedure

1. Talk to the students about the importance of sending clear, sincere messages to other people. As you have already completed a listening activity with the students, point out that speaking is the other half of the communication process. Emphasize that sending a clear message is particularly important when talking to people who are not good listeners. Being heard and understood takes care and effort.

2. Write the steps for I—messages on the board. Underneath the headings, begin to develop examples.

   - Say what is happening—what is causing the problem

     When you ...

     ... take things that belong to me without asking

     ... talk when I am trying to talk

     ... keep the kitten in your room all of the time

   - Say how it affects you

     "I feel ...

     ... irritated because I don't have my things when I need them

     ... frustrated because I can't finish what I am saying

     ... sad because I haven't gotten to play with her

   - Say what you want

     I'd like you to ...

     ... ask me before you take something

     ... listen to me tell my story

     ... share her with me

3. Have students complete their experience sheet, constructing practice I—statements. Invite several students to read their statements to the group. Get the students to think of other typical situations and, together, develop I—statements for each one.

Discussion
1. "What is the most difficult part of sending I—statements?"
2. "How is sending an I—statement more effective than demanding what you want?"
3. "How do you feel when someone blames or criticizes you?"
4. "Are you more likely to listen to an I—statement or a blaming, criticizing message? Why?"

Evaluation
Group members construct at least one I–statement to fit a typical situation in their lives.

Leader Note
Role-play some of the situations. Have the actors try less effective ways of communicating their wishes, such as demanding, whining, criticizing, name calling, etc., and then substitute an I–statement. Discuss the differences in effectiveness (getting the job done) and the impact on the listener and the relationship.

---

* Also available on CD

Note. From *50 Activities for Teaching Emotional Intelligence, Level II: Middle School* (pp. 113–115), by D. Schilling and S. Palomares, 1996, Austin, TX: PRO-ED, Inc. Copyright 1996 by PRO-ED, Inc. Adapted with permission.

Getting Your Message Across

Practice writing I–statements.

You are working in teams in your class. You have some really good ideas about what your team could do, but one person keeps talking whenever you try to tell the group your ideas. You are getting upset, so you decide to use an I–statement.

When you _____ ,

I feel _____ *and I want you*

to _____ .

140

You are trying to study at home. The TV is so loud in the next room that you can't think. You decide to explain how the noise is affecting you.

When you _____ ,

I feel _____ *and I want you*

to _____ .

You have two really good friends, but one of the friends does not want to let your other friend hang out with the two of you. This doesn't seem like the right way to treat a friend so you decide to use an I–statement.

When you _____ ,

I feel _____ *and I want you*

to _____ .

Note. From *50 Activities for Teaching Emotional Intelligence, Level II: Middle School* (p. 115), by D. Schilling and S. Palomares, 1996, Austin, TX: PRO-ED, Inc. Copyright 1996 by PRO-ED, Inc. Adapted with permission.

How to Recognize a Good Listener

Objectives
Group members will recognize and demonstrate the skills of good listening.

Materials
*How to Recognize a Good Listener** experience sheet for each student; pencils or markers

Procedure
1. Complete the experience sheet with the group.
2. Ask for volunteers to be the speaker and the listener. Have them talk for about 1 minute.
3. Have the rest of the group identify examples of good listening.

Discussion
1. "What is your strongest quality as a listener?"
2. "What is your weakest quality as a listener?"
3. "How can you become a better listener?"

Evaluation
Students will describe their listening abilities and make a plan for improving them.

---

* Also available on CD

Note. From *Preparing Teens for the World of Work* (p. 68), by D. Schilling, P. Schwallie-Giddis, and W. J. Giddis, 1995, Austin, TX: PRO-ED, Inc. Copyright 1995 by PRO-ED, Inc. Adapted with permission.

How to Recognize a Good Listener

Listed below are characteristics of a good listener. Check the ones that describe you most of the time.

A good listener:

☐ Faces the speaker.

☐ Looks into the speaker's eyes, but doesn't stare.

☐ Is relaxed, but pays attention.

☐ Keeps an open mind.

☐ Listens to the words and tries to picture what the speaker is saying.

☐ Doesn't interrupt or fidget.

☐ Waits for the speaker to pause before asking questions.

☐ Asks questions only to make sure to understand something that has been said so as not to disrupt the train of thought.

☐ Tries to feel what the speaker is feeling.

☐ Nods and says "Uh huh" or summarizes to let the speaker know he or she is listening.

☐ Pays attention to feelings, facial expressions, gestures, posture, and other nonverbal cues.

Note. From *Preparing Teens for the World of Work* (p. 68), by D. Schilling, P. Schwallie-Giddis, and W. J. Giddis, 1995, Austin, TX: PRO-ED, Inc. Copyright 1995 by PRO-ED, Inc. Adapted with permission.

Name Game

Objectives
Group members will identify ways to compliment others and plan to compliment a specific person.

Materials
Circles of fuzzy material, chenille stems, movable eyes, construction paper cut in circles, glue, scissors, safety pins, *Friendship Wheel** for each student, and markers or crayons

Procedure
1. Explain that a "fuzzy" is a good deed or act. Discuss how giving a fuzzy away is contagious. Name persons to whom students might give a fuzzy.
2. Discuss the different kinds of fuzzies that can be exchanged, such as smiles, favors, and good schoolwork.
3. Have members make two warm fuzzies each out of the materials by attaching arms and legs to the circles and drawing faces. They should make one to wear and one to give away to a friend. When the student gives his fuzzy away, he should tell the person what he likes about him or her.
4. Have the students fill in the *Friendship Wheel* with words or drawings of ways they can be friends to others in their class or in their school.

Discussion
1. "How do you feel when someone pays you a compliment?"
2. "How does it help others when they hear a compliment?"

Evaluation
Students each identify one person they will give their warm fuzzy to and what they will say to that person when they do. Students list or illustrate other ways they can be friends to students in their class.

---

* Also available on CD

Note. From *Child Support Through Small Group Counseling* (p. 180), by L. Landy, 1990, Indianapolis, IN: KIDRIGHTS. Copyright 1990 by KIDRIGHTS. Adapted with permission.

Friendship Wheel

Name _____ Date _____

Think of ways you can be a friend to someone in this group, your class, or this school. Write or draw each friendly deed in a different section of the Friendship Wheel.

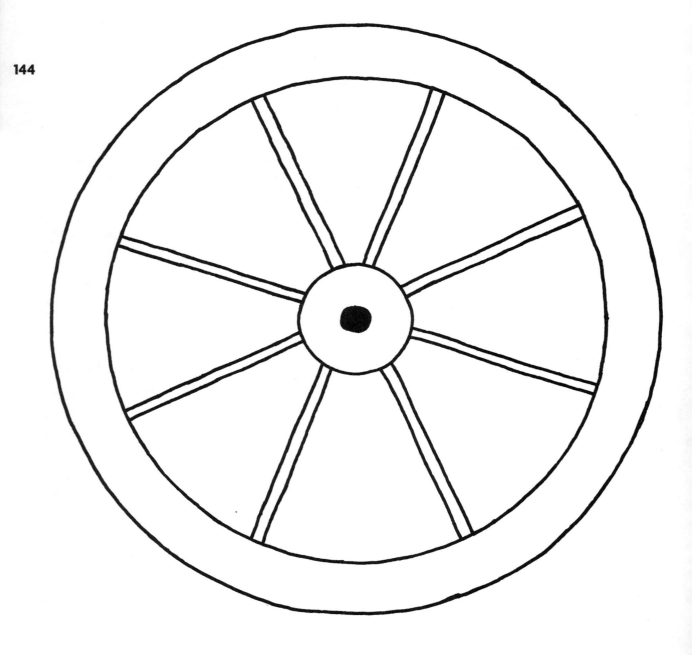

Note. From *Esteem Builders* (p. 199), by M. Borba, 1989, Austin, TX: PRO-ED, Inc. Copyright 1989 by PRO-ED, Inc. Adapted with permission.

I–Messages:
Still No Substitute!

Objectives

The group members will:

1. describe how they typically handle negative feelings in conflict situations,
2. practice formulating and delivering I–messages, and
3. state the benefits of I–messages over other ways of handling negative feelings.

Materials

I–Messages cards*

Procedure

1. Introduce the concept of I–messages. Explain: *Probably the most effective way to deal with negative feelings is to express them honestly and let the other person know what he or she did to cause them. You can do this by using an I–message. An I–message usually begins with the word "I" and has three parts. In the first part you state your feelings ("I feel cheated"); in the second part you describe the behavior that caused your feelings ("… when you eat all the cookies"); and in the third part you explain what you want the person to do ("… and in the future I'd like you to share them with me").*

2. Write the formula for constructing an I–message on the board:

   I feel _____

   when you _____

   and I'd like you to _____

   or

   I feel _____

   because _____

   and I want _____

3. Ask some of the students to try formulating an I–message and pretend to say it to the object of their negative feelings (played by you). Coach the students until they demonstrate that they grasp the concept and the formula.

4. Allow the group to select from the stack of *I–Messages* scenario cards. As each student selects a scenario, have the student respond, and then go around the group, with each student creating an I–message.

Discussion

1. "As the receiver, how did you feel when you heard the I–message?"
2. "As the sender, what was it like to state the I–message?"
3. "Why are I–messages more effective than some of the other ways that we typically handle our negative feelings?"

SOS! *A Practical Guide*

Evaluation

Students will apply the formula to scenarios and a real-life situation. Students will report having used I–messages for the duration of the group.

* Also available on CD

Note. From *Group Activities for Counselors* (pp. 61–63), by S. Elliot, 1994, Austin, TX: PRO-ED, Inc. Copyright 1994 by PRO-ED, Inc. Adapted with permission.

I–Messages

Your parent tells your brother that he can go to the mall with his friends. When you asked to go to the mall just fifteen minutes ago, the same parent told you "no." <div align="right">ICS-I-1</div>	You share a room with your sister. Today was her turn to straighten up and she didn't do it. You are both in danger of being restricted. <div align="right">ICS-I-1</div>
Your friend promises to walk home from school with you. You wait and wait, but your friend never shows up. Walking home by yourself, you meet your friend coming down the sidewalk with another kid. <div align="right">ICS-I-1</div>	You lend your friend five dollars, which she promises to pay back before the end of the week. You need the money for the weekend, but on Friday your friend says she doesn't have it. <div align="right">ICS-I-1</div>
You tell your best friend a secret that no one else knows. In less than a week, three different kids tell you that they know about your secret. When you ask your best friend about it, he shrugs and acts like it's not important. <div align="right">ICS-I-1</div>	You and a partner were assigned to work together on a project. She keeps making excuses for not doing a portion of the work. Soon it will be time to turn in the assignment and you're worried about getting a failing grade. <div align="right">ICS-I-1</div>

Note. From *Group Activities for Counselors* (p. 63), by S. Elliot, 1994, Austin, TX: PRO-ED, Inc. Copyright 1994 by PRO-ED, Inc. Adapted with permission.

The Active Listener

Objectives

Group members will:

1. define the role of the receiver in communication, and
2. identify and demonstrate "active listening" behaviors.

Materials

A diagram of the communication process*; *The Active Listener* poster*; topic cards*

Procedure

1. Using the diagram of the communication process, explain to the group that in order for two people to enjoy and encourage each other, to work, play, or solve problems together, they need to be able to communicate effectively. *In every example of communication, no matter how small, a message is sent from one person (the sender) to the other person (the receiver). The message is supposed to tell the receiver something about the feelings and thoughts of the sender. Because senders cannot give receivers their thoughts and feelings, they have to be "coded" in words. Good communicators pick words that describe their feelings and thoughts as closely as possible. Nonverbal "signals"—for example, a smile, a frown, or a hand gesture—almost always accompany the verbal message. Sometimes the entire message is nonverbal. Good communicators send nonverbal signals that exactly match their feelings and thoughts.*

2. Ask the students to describe what a good receiver says and does to show that he or she is interested in and is really listening to what the sender is saying. Show *The Active Listener* poster to the group and discuss.

3. Tell the students that this kind of listening is called *active listening*. Ask them if they can explain why the word *active* is used to describe this process.

4. Ask the students to form groups of three, designating one student A, another B, and another as C.

5. Give the students an opportunity to practice active listening. *In the first round, A will be the sender. B will be the receiver and will use active listening. C will be the observer. C's job is to notice how well B listens and report his or her observations at the end of the round. I will be the timekeeper. We will have three rounds, so that you can each have a turn in all three roles. When you are the sender, pick a topic from the cards, and remember to pause occasionally so that your partner can respond.*

6. Signal the start of the first round. Call time after three minutes. Have the Cs (observers) give feedback for one minute. Tell the students to switch roles. Conduct two more rounds. Lead a follow-up discussion.

Discussion

1. "How did it feel to 'actively listen'?"
2. "How difficult was it to feel empathy for your partner?"
3. "What was it like to be the observer?"
4. "When you were the sender, how did it feel to have someone really empathize with and listen to you?"

5. "What was easiest about active listening?"

6. "What did you learn from your observer?"

7. "Why is it important to learn to be a good listener?"

Evaluation

Students demonstrate active listening skills in at least one of the communication exercises.

* Also available on CD

Note. From *50 Activities for Teaching Emotional Intelligence, Level II: Middle School* (pp. 97–98), by D. Schilling and S. Palomares, 1996, Austin, TX: PRO-ED, Inc. Copyright 1996 by PRO-ED, Inc. Adapted with permission.

The Communication Process

SENDER　　　　　**RECEIVER**

Note. From *50 Activities for Teaching Emotional Intelligence, Level II: Middle School* (p. 97), by D. Schilling and S. Palomares, 1996, Austin, TX: PRO-ED, Inc. Copyright 1996 by PRO-ED, Inc. Adapted with permission.

The Active Listener

- Face the sender.

- Look into the sender's eyes.

- Be relaxed, but attentive.

- Listen to the words and try to picture in your own mind what the sender is saying.

- Don't interrupt or fidget. When it is your turn to respond, don't change the subject or start telling your own story.

- If you don't understand something, wait for the sender to pause and then ask, "What do you mean by ...?"

- Try to feel what the sender is feeling (show empathy).

- Respond in ways that let the sender know that you are listening and understand what is being said. You can respond with nods, saying "Uh huh," or giving feedback that proves you are listening. For example:

  —Briefly summarize: "You're saying that you might have to quit the team in order to have time for a paper route."

  —Restate feelings, showing empathy: "You must be feeling pretty bad" or "You sound really happy!"

Note. From *50 Activities for Teaching Emotional Intelligence, Level II: Middle School* (p. 99), by D. Schilling and S. Palomares, 1996, Austin, TX: PRO-ED, Inc. Copyright 1996 by PRO-ED, Inc. Adapted with permission.

INTERPERSONAL AND COMMUNICATION SKILLS

151

Topic Cards

152

A Time I Needed Some Help ICS-I-2	Something I'd Like to Do Better ICS-I-2
A Problem I Need to Solve ICS-I-2	A Time I Got Into an Argument ICS-I-2
A Time I Had to Make a Tough Decision ICS-I-2	Something I'd Like to Be or Do When I'm an Adult ICS-I-2

Note. From *50 Activities for Teaching Emotional Intelligence, Level II: Middle School* (p. 98), by D. Schilling and S. Palomares, 1996, Austin, TX: PRO-ED, Inc. Copyright 1996 by PRO-ED, Inc. Adapted with permission.

The Clique Phenomenon

Objectives
Group members will:

1. identify ways to make new friends,
2. define the term *clique* and describe the effects of cliques, and
3. state how they can avoid making other people feel left out.

Materials
Making New Friends poster*; a copy of *Getting On Your Own Side** for each student; chalkboard or chart paper

Procedure
1. Brainstorm with the group to make a list describing as many ways as they can think of to make new friends. Show the *Making New Friends* poster of possible ideas, writing in other ideas from the group.

2. Write the word *clique* on the board and ask the students to help you define it. One possible definition might be "A group of people that defines itself as much by who is excluded as by who is included."

3. Discuss how a clique's policy of exclusion causes members to have difficulty making new friends and can completely frustrate the efforts of someone who is not in the clique to become good friends with someone who is. Emphasize that the reason many kids want to be a part of a clique is that they want to be liked by "important" people and feel important themselves.

4. Ask the students to turn to the experience sheet, *Getting on Your Own Side*. Allow a few minutes for students to complete the sheet. Then ask them to (voluntarily) share their answers to the questions.

5. Encourage the students to commit to making one new friend before the next session or to include one new person in their existing group of friends. Stipulate that before they can claim to have completed this assignment, the students must do something tangible with the new friend, such as sit together at an assembly, eat lunch together, and so forth.

6. Ask the students to pay attention to the clique phenomenon and avoid doing anything that causes another person to feel left out.

Discussion
1. "In what ways do you think cliques are good?"
2. "In what ways do you think cliques are harmful?"
3. "Have you ever wanted to belong to a clique? If so, why was it important?"
4. "What would happen if there were no cliques at this school?"
5. "What kinds of cliques do adults have?"

Evaluation
Students identify harmful effects of cliques, examine their own behavior in contributing to cliques, and make a plan to include rather than exclude other students in their friendship group.

Leader Note

The issues of cliques and power differentials in relationships in schools are very intense. Be sure to know your group members' social issues to be aware of underlying power issues playing out in the group so that group can always be a safe place for everyone. Guard against students' making in-depth disclosures if you believe disclosures will put them at risk of embarrassment or ridicule. As always, maintaining confidentiality and the No Put-Down rule are very important.

* Also available on CD

Note. From *50 Activities for Teaching Emotional Intelligence, Level III: High School* (pp. 98–99), by D. Schilling and S. Palomares, 1999, Austin, TX: PRO-ED, Inc. Copyright 1999 by PRO-ED, Inc. Adapted with permission.

Making New Friends

Sit beside someone different in the cafeteria and say hello	Offer to show someone new around the school	Join a school organization	Offer to help someone carry a heavy load
Team up with someone you don't know very well to work on a class project	Run an ad in the school paper asking for a companion for activities like hiking or bicycling	Ask someone you know to introduce you to new people	Go to the gym or track after school and say hello to the kids who are there

Note. From *50 Activities for Teaching Emotional Intelligence, Level III: High School* (pp. 98–99), by D. Schilling and S. Palomares, 1999, Austin, TX: PRO-ED, Inc. Copyright 1999 by PRO-ED, Inc. Adapted with permission.

SOS! *A Practical Guide*

Getting On Your Own Side

Is it worth it to be "in"?

What have you done to be included in a group?

I have ...

YES	NO	Risked losing friends
YES	NO	Hurt people who thought they were my friends by making them feel left out
YES	NO	Done something I thought was not right
YES	NO	Taken drugs or alcohol
YES	NO	Done something that might have harmed me physically
YES	NO	Done something that cost me a lot of money
YES	NO	Done something that interfered with my schoolwork
YES	NO	Done something that my parents would have objected to if they had known
YES	NO	Done whatever was necessary, as long as it didn't harm anyone else
YES	NO	Done something that was against my religion
YES	NO	Done whatever was necessary

Can you remember a time when you were pressured to exclude someone from an activity? How did you feel?

_____

_____

What did you do?

_____

_____

If this ever happens again, what do you think you will do?

_____

_____

Note. From *50 Activities for Teaching Emotional Intelligence, Level III: High School* (p. 100), by D. Schilling and S. Palomares, 1999, Austin, TX: PRO-ED, Inc. Copyright 1999 by PRO-ED, Inc. Adapted with permission.

INTERPERSONAL AND COMMUNICATION SKILLS

The ASSERT Formula

Objectives
The group members will:

1. identify their rights in interpersonal situations,
2. identify ways to communicate assertively using oral and nonverbal language, and
3. practice making I–statements.

Materials
Student Bill of Rights poster*; *Watch Your Body Language* poster*; a copy of the ASSERT Formula card for each student*

Procedure
1. Talk to the students about the differences in aggressive, passive, and assertive behaviors. *Bullies tend to be aggressive—they behave as if their rights matter more than anyone else's rights. Victims tend to be passive—they behave as if other people's rights matter more than theirs. Assertive people respect their own rights and other people's rights.*
2. Show students the *Student Bill of Rights* poster. Add other rights they offer.
3. Show students the *Watch Your Body Language* poster and talk about how body language contributes to being assertive. *Pair assertive body language with assertive words, spoken in a firm, confident, determined voice. Don't mumble or whine—but don't shout either. Say what you mean and mean what you say.*
4. Distribute the ASSERT Formula cards and lead the students through the steps. Have them practice the formula with their suggested situations.

Discussion
1. "What behaviors have you noticed in other assertive people?"
2. "Describe a time when you were assertive."
3. "How were you able to do that even in a tough situation?"
4. "What will help you to be assertive the next time you feel your rights have been violated?"
5. "What would you tell someone who was struggling with being assertive about how to do it?"

Evaluation
Students demonstrate the ASSERT Formula in real-life situations. They make a plan of communicating assertively rather than aggressively or passively.

Leader Note
Students who are naturally shy and withdrawn and those who have been (or are) bullying targets will need extra help learning and using assertiveness skills. Students need to understand that bullying is a behavior that will not be tolerated and for which there are disciplinary

consequences. Avoid mediating a bullying episode between two students. Because of the power differential that exists between a bully and his or her target, mediating can strengthen the bully's position and increase the effect on the target student. Enforce group agreements about put-downs and treating all members with respect.

* Also available on CD

Note. From *Bully Free Classroom* (pp. 52–55), by A. L. Beane, 1999, Minneapolis, MN: Free Spirit Publishing Inc. Copyright 1999 by Free Spirit Publishing Inc. Adapted with permission.

SOS! *A Practical Guide*

STUDENT BILL OF RIGHTS

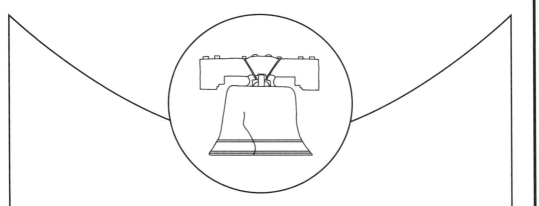

1. We have the right to think for ourselves.

2. We have the right to have and express our opinions, views, and beliefs.

3. We have the right to make decisions about our lives.

4. We have the right to say "no."

5. We have the right to say "yes."

6. We have the right to stand up to people who tease us, criticize us, or put us down.

7. We have the right to have and express our feelings.

8. We have the right to respond when someone violates our rights.

9. _____

10. _____

Note. From *Bully Free Classroom* (p. 53), by A. L. Beane, 1999, Minneapolis, MN: Free Spirit Publishing Inc. Copyright 1999 by Free Spirit Publishing Inc. Adapted with permission.

Watch Your Body Language

160

Five Basics of Assertive Body Language:

1. Stand up straight. Stand with your feet slightly apart so that you feel balanced and stable.

2. Keep your head up.

3. Keep you shoulders straight. Don't hunch.

4. Look people in the eye—not over their heads, not at the ground—right in the eye.

5. Don't back off when you're talking to someone. Move closer—but not too close. Keep a comfortable distance between you.

When you *look* assertive,
you're more likely to *feel* assertive.
People are more likely to treat you with respect.

Note. From *Bully Free Classroom* (p. 53), by A. L. Beane, 1999, Minneapolis, MN: Free Spirit Publishing Inc. Copyright 1999 by Free Spirit Publishing Inc. Adapted with permission.

The ASSERT Formula

A = *Attention.* Before you can talk about and try to solve a problem, you need to get the person's attention. *Sean, I need to talk to you about something. Is now a good time?*

S = *Soon, Simple, and Short.* Speak up as soon as you realize your rights have been violated. Look the person in the eye and keep your comments brief and to the point. *It's about something that happened in the hall today.*

S = *Specific Behavior.* What did the person do to violate your rights? Focus on the behavior, not the person. Be as specific as you can. *I didn't like it when you pushed against my locker, I dropped my books, and you kicked them across the hall.*

E = *Effect on Me.* Share what you experienced as a result of the person's behavior. *I was late for class. I had to wait for the hall to clear to pick up my books.*

R = *Response.* Wait for a response from the other person. He or she may try to brush you off with "What's the big deal?" or "Don't be a baby" or "Can't you take a joke?" or "So what?" Don't let it bother you. At least it's a response. On the other hand, the person might apologize when he or she learns that you will speak up when your rights are violated.

T = *Terms.* Suggest a solution to the problem. *I want you to stop bothering me in the hall. If you don't, I'll report it.*

Tip: Some bullies feed on getting any kind of response, even an assertive response. If your being assertive seems to provoke the bully, walk away and report it.

SOS! *A Practical Guide*

161

INTERPERSONAL AND COMMUNICATION SKILLS

Mastering Assertive Communication

Objectives

Group members will:

1. describe the differences between assertive, aggressive, and passive behaviors;

2. practice assertive and nonassertive behaviors in role-play situations; and

3. explain how assertive, aggressive, and passive behaviors affect situations involving harassment.

Materials

Communication Styles poster*; *Acting Assertively* scenario cards*

Procedure

1. Begin by talking with the students about the choice they have to communicate passively, aggressively, or assertively. Point out that sometimes people act passively or aggressively because they haven't learned how to be assertive. When this is the case it is difficult for people to get their needs met or their ideas expressed.

2. Display the *Communication Styles* poster. Read the definitions of "aggressive," "passive," and "assertive" together.

3. Discuss the differences. Give some examples from your own experience.

4. Have each student pick from the stack of *Acting Assertively* scenario cards. Solicit input from the group to decide:

    a. Which responses are passive, aggressive, and assertive?

    b. What personal rights are being violated by each aggressive response?

    c. What personal rights are being violated by each passive response?

5. Invite some pairs to role-play the different situations. Have them role-play all three responses, and then discuss the differences between the three. Facilitate discussion throughout the role plays.

Discussion

1. "How did you feel when you were being aggressive? ... passive? ... assertive?"

2. "How did you feel when you were on the receiving end of an aggressive response? ... a passive response? ... an assertive response?"

3. "How do you react when someone almost always responds aggressively but disguises his or her responses with attempts at humor?"

4. "What is going on when people respond passively?"

5. "Which kind of behavior is being demonstrated by harassment of any kind?"

6. "When you ignore incidents of sexual harassment, what kind of message are you giving the harasser?"

7. "What skills do you need to practice to become comfortably assertive?"

Evaluation

Students identify situations that include aggressive communication in their lives and discuss assertive responses they will be comfortable in making.

Leader Note

Help students to understand the influence of tone of voice and nonverbal communication in sending an aggressive, passive, or assertive message. Be sure you understand the laws and policies regarding reporting harassment so that you can inform and support your students should harassment be an issue for any group member.

* Also available on CD

Note. From *Group Activities for Counselors* (p. 182), by S. Eliot, 1994, Austin, TX: PRO-ED, Inc. Copyright 1994 by PRO-ED, Inc. Adapted with permission.

Communication Styles

What does it mean to communicate in an aggressive, passive, or assertive way?

Aggressive communication:

- Intentionally attacks, takes advantage of, humiliates, hurts, harasses, retaliates, or puts down others
- Is action based on the belief that others are not as important as the speaker

S → R

Passive communication:

- Invites, encourages, or permits others to take advantage of or harass the speaker
- Discounts the speaker and portrays others as more important than the speaker is

_S → **R**

Assertive communication:

- Is an open and honest expression used to communicate needs, wants, or feelings without demanding or discounting the wants, needs, or feelings of others
- Is action based on the belief that all people, including the speaker, are equally important and deserving of respect

S → R

Note. From *Group Activities for Counselors* (p. 184), by S. Elliot, 1994, Austin, TX: PRO-ED, Inc. Copyright 1994 by PRO-ED, Inc. Adapted with permission.

Sylvia starts flirting with Brad during lunch. At first, he's flattered, but when she starts hanging on him, he backs off. But Sylvia won't leave him alone. Finally, Brad responds:

1. "Sylvia, I feel really crowded when you come on to me that way. I'm not interested, so please don't do it anymore."
2. "Uh, err, gee, Sylvia. What's gotten into you?"
3. by pushing Sylvia away and yelling, "Get out of here, Ugly. I don't want you!"

ICS-S-2

Natalie drives into the parking lot of a small mall, but all of the handicapped spaces are taken, so she has to park in a regular spot and then struggle to remove her chair from the back seat. As she's passing one of the handicapped spaces, Natalie almost collides with a young guy running to his car. She says:

1. "Thanks to you, Mister, I just had to struggle for 20 minutes getting out of my car. Maybe when you pay a fine, you'll stop being so selfish."
2. "Hi. I guess maybe you didn't notice that's a handicapped spot?"
3. "You violate my rights when you take a spot that's reserved for people with disabilities. I hope you won't do it again."

ICS-S-2

Julian offers to fix the chain on Raquel's bike. When she thanks him, he replies, "If you really want to thank me, come here and give me a kiss." Raquel responds:

1. "I'd rather kiss a hyena than a jerk like you. Get out of my face!"
2. "I feel tricked when you offer to help me and then expect something in return. If 'thank you' isn't enough, please don't offer to help me again."
3. by making a face and riding off on her bike.

ICS-S-2

Andy returns a pair of jeans to the store because the zipper is broken. The clerk says:

1. "Yes, that's a broken zipper all right. Can I get you another pair?"
2. "Oh, I'm so sorry. I should have checked the jeans before I sold them to you. It's all my fault."
3. "You broke this zipper, didn't you? Well, you're not going to cheat us!"

ICS-S-2

(continues)

166

Marcia is walking down the hall when Hal comes up beside her, puts his arm around her waist, and whispers in her ear, "You look really good today, Marcia." Marcia stops and says:

1. "Excuse me, Hal. I hear my mother calling."
2. "Hal, I am a person, not a pretzel. I'd appreciate it if you would keep your hands off me and treat me with a little respect."
3. "Get your filthy hands off me, you pervert, or you won't have any teeth left in your mouth!"

ICS-S-2

Lydia insists that Jennifer carry some things to the gym for her. Jennifer responds:

1. "I'm afraid I'll be late for English, but if you want me to, okay."
2. "What's the matter with you? Are your arms broken?"
3. "I can't help you right now, Lydia. I have to get to my English class."

ICS-S-2

Tina has to pass a group of guys on her way to class. As she walks by, they start a chorus of sounds and gestures that cause Tina to see red. She responds:

1. by looking straight ahead and hurrying past.
2. by making a gesture of her own and then walking over and slapping one of the guys across the face.
3. "I have a right to use this hallway without getting any grief from you. If you ever do that to me again, I'll report you."

ICS-S-2

Will loaned his friend Sam some money for gas. Sam promised to pay it back before the weekend. Now it is Friday afternoon and Will asks him to repay the loan. Sam responds:

1. "You are such a whiner! You'd think I stole your car! I'll pay you when I pay you!"
2. "I am the biggest jerk for not remembering. I hope you can forgive me!"
3. "Sure, man, here's the cash. Thanks for helping me out!"

ICS-S-2

Note. From *Group Activities for Counselors* (pp. 184–185), by S. Elliot, 1994, Austin, TX: PRO-ED, Inc. Copyright 1994 by PRO-ED, Inc. Adapted with permission.

Group Discussion Roles

Objective
Group members will develop listening and speaking skills to enhance communication.

Materials
Group Discussion Roles poster*; 6 role cards*; *Leader Issue Scenario* cards*

Procedure
1. Display the *Group Discussion Roles* poster and discuss the meaning of the four communication roles.
2. Have students give examples of situations that describe each role.
3. Have each group member select a role card and then a scenario.
4. Role-play the first scenario discussion for a few minutes with each group member staying in his or her selected role. Ask the students to identify which role each student was playing and how they know.
5. Have the students return the role cards to the pile, select again, and role-play the second scenario discussion.
6. Repeat with a scenario of the group's choice.

Discussion
1. "How do these roles enhance or inhibit interaction and problem solving in the group?"
2. "How do people develop these roles in group situations where the roles are not assigned but are assumed by the participants?"
3. "Sometimes discussion groups have problems. Knowing these roles, how can members help the group reach a problem resolution?"

Evaluation
Students describe the four major roles that develop during group interaction: leader, listener, gatekeeper, and advocate.

Leader Note
Explain how these are roles that help group discussion. One person can play a single role or more than one role at the same time.

* Also available on CD

Note. From *Developmental Guidance Classroom Activities for Use with National Career Development Guidelines, Grades 10–12* (#90), by J. A. Rogala, R. Lambert, and K. Verhage, 1992, Madison, WI: Center on Education and Work. Copyright 1992 by Center on Education and Work. Adapted with permission.

-3a # Group Discussion Roles

Leader

Speak up. You have something to say and it is important. Say it so that everyone can hear it.

Take the risk. People get scared about speaking up sometimes for fear others will laugh at them or think what they say is dumb. The more ideas people hear, the more informed they will be, which will help them make better decisions.

Tell how you feel and why. There is a lot of difference between saying, "I hate baseball because I don't play well," and saying, "Baseball is a stupid game!" In the first statement, you give a personal reason for your feelings. In the second, you make it sound as if everyone should feel the same way.

Listener

Look at the speaker. Looking at the speaker helps him or her know we are listening.

Repeat how the other person feels and why. It is important that people know you are listening to them and that you understand them.

Gatekeeper

Be an observer. The gatekeeper opens the gate and helps others come into the conversation.

Show concern. The gatekeeper is first an observer, seeing who is being left out and showing concern. The gatekeeper welcomes that person by opening the gate and inviting him or her to come in.

Tell how you feel when others are left out and why. The gatekeeper tells the person being left out, "I'm worried you might not have had a chance to speak. What ideas would you like to share?"

Advocate

Support the group. An advocate speaks up in support of the group so that the discussion is a good one. The advocate speaks up when someone is disruptive or playing, whispering, or not showing concern.

Give feedback. An advocate gives feedback by telling others how he or she feels, and also speaks up to point out to the group what members are doing that is working to make a good discussion and a good problem-solving experience.

Note. From *Developmental Guidance Classroom Activities for Use with National Career Development Guidelines, Grades 10–12* (#90), by J. A. Rogala, R. Lambert, and K. Verhage, 1992, Madison, WI: Center on Education and Work. Copyright 1992 by Center on Education and Work. Adapted with permission.

Role Cards

Leader

You start the discussion. You have a problem you want to risk talking about. You want to tell the group how you feel about the problem.

ICS-S-3

Listener

Look at the speaker.

Repeat how the speaker feels and why.

ICS-S-3

Gatekeeper

Observe the group's discussion.

Show concern.

Invite others into the discussion.

ICS-S-3

Advocate

Support the group.

Give feedback when you see behaviors that help and behaviors that don't help.

ICS-S-3

Distractor

Whisper your feelings to the person next to you instead of saying them out loud.

ICS-S-3

Nontalker

Act shy.

ICS-S-3

Note. From *Developmental Guidance Classroom Activities for Use with National Career Development Guidelines, Grades 10–12* (#90), by J. A. Rogala, R. Lambert, and K. Verhage, 1992, Madison, WI: Center on Education and Work. Copyright 1992 by Center on Education and Work. Adapted with permission.

Leader Issue Scenario Cards

CHEATING

Your issue concerns the cheating that goes on when you play ball. You are really mad at some of your friends because they are not playing fair and then they try to act "big" when they get away with it. You want to tell the group how you feel about it and figure out a way to have fair ball games.

ICS-S-3

FRIENDS REFUSE TO SPEAK TO EACH OTHER

You have two friends who will not speak to each other. If you are nice to one of them, the other one will get mad at you. You do not know what to do but you do know that you want to be able to be friends with both of these people and you want them to treat each other respectfully.

ICS-S-3

CREATE YOUR OWN ISSUE

_____

_____

_____

_____

_____

_____

ICS-S-3

Note. From *Developmental Guidance Classroom Activities for Use with National Career Development Guidelines, Grades 10–12* (#90), by J. A. Rogala, R. Lambert, and K. Verhage, 1992, Madison, WI: Center on Education and Work. Copyright 1992 by Center on Education and Work. Adapted with permission.

Accepting Responsibility
Versus Blaming Others

Objective
Group members will be able to accept responsibility for their actions without blaming others.

Materials
Accepting Responsibility Versus Blaming Others poster*; *Responsibility* cards*; *Choosing the Best Response* page*

Procedure
1. Discuss doing something that someone talks you into (breaking a rule, stealing, disobeying a parent) and that gets you into trouble. Help students see when their behavior is their responsibility. Discuss blaming others for our mistakes.
2. Using the *Accepting Responsibility* poster, review the strategies.
3. Use the *Responsibility* cards or ask the students to role-play a common problem, decide who caused the problem, and select a correct response. Give feedback. You may use the blanks to write common problems.
4. Talk about responsibility. Responsibility is acknowledging one's own power to choose how to act.
5. Give students the *Response* page to work on a problem.

Discussion
1. "How is the response you chose showing your power to choose how to act?"
2. "How does making responsible choices help us and others?"

Evaluation
Students will identify responsible choices in typical problem situations.

171

RESPONSIBLE BEHAVIOR

---

* Also available on CD

Note. From *Getting to Know You! Social Skills Curriculum for Grades 1–3* (pp. 161–162), by D. Hanken and J. Kennedy, 1998, Minneapolis, MN: Educational Media Corporation. Copyright 1998 by Educational Media Corporation. Adapted with permission.

SOS! *A Practical Guide*

Accepting Responsibility
Versus Blaming Others

172

1. Identify the problem.

2. Did I cause it?

3. Choose a response.

A. Apologize.

B. Replace it.

C. Tell the truth.

Note. From *Getting to Know You! Social Skills Curriculum for Grades 1–3* (p. 162), by D. Hanken and J. Kennedy, 1998, Minneapolis, MN: Educational Media Corporation. Copyright 1998 by Educational Media Corporation. Adapted with permission.

RESPONSIBLE BEHAVIOR

Responsibility Cards

You fail a math test because you did not study but you tell your parents you failed the test because the test was not fair.

RB-P-1

You forget your homework and your lunch money. Whose responsibility is it?

RB-P-1

You blame your sister or brother for starting a fight.

RB-P-1

Your friend is always teasing you, so you call him a name.

RB-P-1

RB-P-1

RB-P-1

173

RESPONSIBLE BEHAVIOR

Note. From *Getting to Know You! Social Skills Curriculum for Grades 1–3* (p. 161), by D. Hanken and J. Kennedy, 1998, Minneapolis, MN: Educational Media Corporation. Copyright 1998 by Educational Media Corporation. Adapted with permission.

Choosing the Best Response

1. Write about a problem. Example: A friend accuses you of tattling to the teacher.
2. Write who caused the problem.
3. Draw one response you could make.
4. Draw another response you could make. *Tell us which is the best response.*

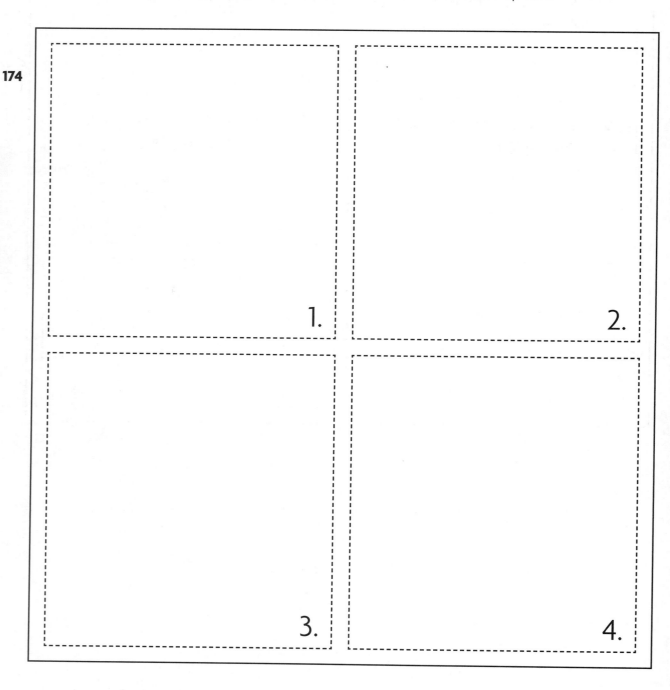

1.

2.

3.

4.

Note. From *Getting to Know You! Social Skills Curriculum for Grades 1–3* (p. 161), by D. Hanken and J. Kennedy, 1998, Minneapolis, MN: Educational Media Corporation. Copyright 1998 by Educational Media Corporation. Adapted with permission.

Welcome to Manners Land!

Objectives

Group members will:

1. determine whether manners are being used in various situations, and
2. demonstrate the use of appropriate, respectful manners in simulated situations.

Materials

Manners Land cards*

Procedure

1. Talk to the students about the reasons we have rules called "manners."
2. Using the *Manners Land* cards, have each student select a card. Read or have the student read the card. Ask students to show a thumbs-up sign if they think the card is an example of good manners. Ask the follow-up question and ask for a demonstration of polite behavior for each card. Allow students to ask for help from the group in demonstrating polite behavior.
3. Continue through all 10 cards.

Manners Land Cards Follow-Up Questions:

1. *What might people think if you do not excuse yourself for burping? Show what you can say to be polite if you accidentally burp.*
2. *What might people think if you don't say "Excuse me"? Show what you can say if you accidentally bump into someone.*
3. *Why is it important to say "Please" when you ask for something? Show how you can politely ask for a piece of gum.*
4. *How might your friend's parents feel about you if you use appropriate manners? Show how you can politely ask for a drink of water.*
5. *Why is it not polite to talk when you should be listening? Show the body talk you could use to listen politely.*
6. *How might your grandparents feel when you use respectful manners? Show how you can politely ask for some cake.*
7. *Why is it polite to wait your turn in line? Show how you can wait your turn in line.*
8. *What might your friend's father think about you if you don't say "Thank you"? Show how you can thank a friend's parent for a ride.*
9. *Why is it important to use table manners at home? Show how you can politely ask your brother to pass the milk.*
10. *Why is it polite to say "You're welcome" when someone thanks you? Show how you can say "You're welcome" to your friend.*

SOS! *A Practical Guide*

Discussion

1. "How do people feel when we treat them politely?"

2. "When we treat other people politely, how can that help us?"

Evaluation

Students identify appropriate manners in a variety of situations.

RESPONSIBLE BEHAVIOR

---

* Also available on CD

Note. From *Social Star* (pp. 270–273), by N. Gajewski, 1993, Eau Claire, WI: Thinking Publications. Copyright 1993 by Thinking Publications. Adapted with permission.

Manners Land

1. You burped loudly and forgot to say "Excuse me."

   RB-P-2

2. When you bumped into a man at the store, you did not say anything to him.

   RB-P-2

3. You forgot to say "Please" when you asked your sister for a piece of gum.

   RB-P-2

4. You asked politely for a drink of water at your friend's house.

   RB-P-2

5. On a field trip, you were talking to others while the leader was talking.

   RB-P-2

6. You said "Please" when you asked your grandfather for some cake.

   RB-P-2

RESPONSIBLE BEHAVIOR

7. You stood in line for a ride at the park. You did not cut into line.

   RB-P-2

8. You said "Thank you" when your friend's father gave you a ride home.

   RB-P-2

9. You said "Please" when you asked your brother to pass the milk during dinner.

   RB-P-2

10. When your friend thanked you for helping, you said "You're welcome."

    RB-P-2

Note. From *Social Star* (p. 270), by N. Gajewski, 1993, Eau Claire, WI: Thinking Publications. Copyright 1993 by Thinking Publications. Adapted with permission.

Something I've Done to Improve Our World

Objective
Group members will describe ways in which they can be responsible for contributing to the betterment of their community and their world.

Materials
Improving the World cards*

Procedure
1. Say to the students: *The topic for this session is "Something I've Done (or Could Do) To Improve Our World (School, Neighborhood)." Can you think of a time when you did something to help others? Can you think of something you could do?*
2. Using the *Improving the World* cards, have students select one and respond from their experience.

Discussion
1. "How do you feel when you do something that helps improve our world?"
2. "How were you able to do that?"
3. "How can you make it happen even more often?"

Evaluation
Students can talk about times they have helped others or identify ways they could help others.

---

* Also available on CD

Note. From *50 Activities for Teaching Emotional Intelligence, Level III: High School* (pp. 95–96), by D. Schilling and S. Palomares, 1999, Austin, TX: PRO-ED, Inc. Copyright 1999 by PRO-ED, Inc. Adapted with permission.

Improving Our World

A Time I Kept My Promise RB-P-3	How I Help at School RB-P-3
How I Show That I'm a Good Citizen RB-P-3	How I Show Respect Toward Others RB-P-3
A Time I Helped Without Being Asked RB-P-3	A Time I Kept a Promise That Was Hard to Keep RB-P-3
A Time I Admitted That I Did It RB-P-3	A Time I Faced a Problem on My Own RB-P-3
A Time I Told the Truth and Was Glad RB-P-3	A Time I Kept an Agreement RB-P-3

RESPONSIBLE BEHAVIOR

Note. From *50 Activities for Teaching Emotional Intelligence, Level III: High School* (pp. 95–96), by D. Schilling and S. Palomares, 1999, Austin, TX: PRO-ED, Inc. Copyright 1999 by PRO-ED, Inc. Adapted with permission.

Steps for Solving a Problem Responsibly

Objective
Group members will develop and practice a process for effective problem solving.

Materials
One copy of *Steps for Solving a Problem Responsibly** for each student

180

Procedure
1. Distribute the copies of *Steps for Solving a Problem Responsibly*.
2. Ask the students to read each step with you and to write notes on their sheet. Generate discussion questions after each step.
3. Introduce a personal example (a problem you need to solve) and take it through the process as part of the discussion.

Discussion
1. Stop all blaming.

   What happens when you get bogged down in the blaming game?

   What are people who constantly blame others for their problems trying to avoid?

   How is blaming others the same as giving away your power?

   When we think of how we want things to be instead of what is wrong in a situation, how does that help?

2. Define the problem.

   Why is it so important to know exactly what the problem is?

   Why does it matter whether it's yours or someone else's?

   When should people not be left to solve their own problems?

   What can happen when a person gets all worked up about a problem that isn't even his or hers?

3. Consider asking for help.

   When is it wise to ask for help?

   Who gets to decide what kind of help you need?

   If what you want is information or advice, and instead the person tries to solve the problem for you, what can you do?

4. Think of alternative solutions.

   What is the advantage of thinking of alternatives?

   If you can't think of more than one or two alternatives, what should you definitely do before making a decision?

   How does collecting information expand your alternatives?

5. Evaluate the alternatives.

   What are some of the ways of collecting information?

   Why not just do the first thing that comes to mind?

   Why is it important to imagine what will happen as a result of trying each alternative?

6. Make a decision.

   If you still can't make a decision, which steps should you return to?

7. Follow through.

   Why stick to a decision?

   What can you do if the solution doesn't work or more problems come up?

   How can you evaluate your decision?

Evaluation

Students can illustrate application of the problem-solving process to at least one real-life problem situation they are facing.

---

* Also available on CD

Note. From *Activities for Counseling Underachievers* (pp. 67–69), by J. Bleuer, S. Palomares, and G. Walz, 1993, Austin, TX: PRO-ED, Inc. Copyright 1993 by PRO-ED, Inc. Adapted with permission.

Steps for Solving a Problem Responsibly

1. *Stop all blaming.*

   It will help me to understand that blaming someone for the problem will not solve it. If I really want to solve the problem, I need to put my energy into working out a solution. Blaming myself and others is a waste of time.

2. *Define the problem.*

   Next, I need to ask myself two questions to help me get started. "What exactly is the problem?" and "Whose problem is it?" If I find that it's not my problem, the best thing I can do is let the people who "own" the problem solve it themselves. Or I can ask them, "How can I help you?"

3. *Consider asking for help.*

   Once I'm sure I "own" the problem and know what it is, I may choose to ask someone for help. For example, I may decide to talk over the problem with someone.

4. *Think of alternative solutions.*

   I need to ask myself, "What are some things I could do about this?" I need to think of as many reasonable ideas for solving the problem as I can. To do this, I will probably need to collect some information.

5. *Evaluate the alternatives.*

   Next, for each idea I come up with I need to ask myself: "What will happen to me and the other people involved if I try this one?" I need to be very honest with myself. If I don't know how someone else would be affected, I need to ask that person, "How will you feel about it if I ... ?"

6. *Make a decision.*

   I need to choose the alternative that has the best chance of succeeding. If my solution is a responsible one, it will not hurt anyone unnecessarily—and it will probably work.

7. *Follow through.*

   After I've made the decision, I'll stick to it for a reasonable length of time. If the decision doesn't work, I'll try another alternative. If the decision works, but causes more problems in the process, I'll start over again to solve them. *And I'll try not to blame myself or anybody else for those problems.*

182

RESPONSIBLE BEHAVIOR

Note. From *Activities for Counseling Underachievers* (pp. 68–69), by J. Bleuer, S. Palomares, and G. Walz, 1993, Austin, TX: PRO-ED, Inc. Copyright 1993 by PRO-ED, Inc. Adapted with permission.

Manners Land: Intermediate

Objectives

Group members will:

1. determine whether manners are being used in various situations, and
2. demonstrate the use of appropriate, respectful manners.

Materials

Manners Land cards*

Procedure

1. Talk to the students about the reasons we have rules called "manners."
2. Using the *Manners Land* cards, have each student select a card. Read or have the student read the card. Ask students to show a thumbs-up sign if they think the card is an example of good manners. Ask the follow-up question and ask for a demonstration of polite behavior for each card. Allow students to ask for help from the group in demonstrating polite behavior.
3. Continue through all 10 cards.

Manners Land Cards Follow-Up Questions:

1. *What might your friend and friend's family think if you get a drink from the refrigerator without asking? Show how you can politely ask for something to drink.*
2. *How might the teacher have felt if you had said, "Yuck, I don't like those"? Show how to say "No, thank you" in a polite way.*
3. *Why is it polite to offer the last piece of something to someone else? Show how to politely offer the last of something to another person.*
4. *Tell why it is polite to say "I'm sorry" when something happens accidentally. Show how to politely say "I'm sorry" for getting your friend's shirt dirty.*
5. *Why might your grandparents feel upset when you jump on their furniture? Show how you can politely sit on a couch.*
6. *Why is it polite to be quiet at a movie? Show how you can sit quietly while watching a movie.*
7. *Why is it polite to walk in line quietly without touching others? Show how you can walk quietly and keep you hands to yourself.*
8. *Why is it polite to wait for others to leave an elevator before boarding? Show how you can wait and enter safely.*
9. *Why is it polite to ask others to pass something that you want? Show how you can politely ask for the dessert to be passed to you.*
10. *Why is it polite to apologize when others' property is damaged by your action? Show how you can apologize and offer to help fix the damage.*

Discussion

1. "How do people feel when we treat them politely?"

2. "When we treat other people politely, how can that help us?"

Evaluation

Students identify appropriate manners in a variety of situations.

---

* Also available on CD

Note. From *Social Star* (p. 273), by N. Gajewski, 1993, Eau Claire, WI: Thinking Publications. Copyright 1993 by Thinking Publications. Adapted with permission.

Manners Land

---

1. At your friend's house, you took a drink out of the refrigerator without asking.

   RB-I-2

2. The teacher brought treats to class. You didn't like the treat so you politely said, "No, thank you."

   RB-I-2

3. There was only one cookie left. You told your brother he could have it.

   RB-I-2

4. You said you were sorry when you accidentally got your friend's shirt dirty.

   RB-I-2

5. You jumped on the couch at your grandparents' house.

   RB-I-2

6. You were quiet at the movie so other people could hear.

   RB-I-2

7. You were walking down the hall from your classroom to the cafeteria. You kept your hands to yourself and your voice quiet.

   RB-I-2

8. You were waiting with your mom to get on an elevator. When the door opened you made sure to give the people getting off the elevator plenty of room to get off before you boarded.

   RB-I-2

9. You are eating dinner at your aunt's house and the dessert you would like is across the table. You say, "Please pass me the dessert."

   RB-I-2

10. Your ball game got out of hand and a ball crashed into the neighbor's flowers. You apologize and offer to help repair the damage.

    RB-I-2

185

RESPONSIBLE BEHAVIOR

Note. From *Social Star* (p. 271), by N. Gajewski, 1993, Eau Claire, WI: Thinking Publications. Copyright 1993 by Thinking Publications. Adapted with permission.

SOS! *A Practical Guide*

Have to ... Choose to ...

Objectives

Group members will:

1. contrast the attitude of being compelled to do something with the attitude of choosing to do it, and

2. describe the feelings associated with taking responsibility for their actions.

Materials

One copy of *Have to ... Choose to* experience sheet* for each student

Procedure

1. Distribute the *Have to ... Choose to* sheets. Ask the students to create a list of things they feel they *have* to do, such as homework, chores, going to school, and so forth.

2. Have students share the list with a partner.

3. Next, tell the students to draw a line through the word *have* in each statement and write the word *choose* in its place. Have the students read the list to their partner again.

4. Expect disagreements concerning what the students *have to do* and what they *choose to do*. Ask what consequences they would face if they didn't do some of the things they listed. Point out that they choose to do many of these things to avoid the consequences.

5. In the spaces at the bottom of the activity sheet, have the students write in some positive self-talk statements describing their freedom of choice. For example, "I freely choose every action I take," or "No one forces me to do anything. I am responsible for my choices."

Discussion

1. "How do your feelings differ when you say 'I choose to ...' from when you say '... have to ...' in talking about your responsibilities?"

2. "How much of a choice do you really have about the things you listed?"

3. "What have you learned about responsibility from this activity?"

Evaluation

Students will articulate the role choice plays in their actions.

Leader Notes

1. Often, students express the belief that they have little choice concerning their day-to-day activities. They point to the expectations of parents, teachers, and "the system" as justification for this belief. Some students feel victimized and powerless.

2. This activity gives students an opportunity to recognize that they do have choices, and to understand how negative self-talk undermines their power and control.

3. When the students recognize that at some level they are indeed choosing their actions, they will experience a greater sense of control in their lives.

---

* Also available on CD

Note. From *50 Activities for Teaching Emotional Intelligence, Level II: Middle School* (pp. 84–85), by D. Schilling and S. Palomares, 1996, Austin, TX: PRO-ED, Inc. Copyright 1996 by PRO-ED, Inc. Adapted with permission.

Have to ... Choose to
Experience Sheet

Make a list of things you think you *have* to do. Be as specific as possible.

Examples:

I have to do my math homework.

I have to take out the trash at home.

I have to arrive at school before 8:00 A.M.

187

1. I have to _____.

2. I have to _____.

3. I have to _____.

4. I have to _____.

5. I have to _____.

6. I have to _____.

Make a list of positive self-talk statements.

1. _____.

2. _____.

3. _____.

4. _____.

Note. From *50 Activities for Teaching Emotional Intelligence, Level II: Middle School* (p. 85), by D. Schilling and S. Palomares, 1996, Austin, TX: PRO-ED, Inc. Copyright 1996 by PRO-ED, Inc. Adapted with permission.

RESPONSIBLE BEHAVIOR

Improving the Study Habit

Objectives

Group members will:

1. learn and practice effective study habits, and

2. develop and implement plans for self-improvement.

Materials

Study Skills Assessment*; Study Skills and Habits poster*; chalkboard or chart tablet

Procedure

1. Begin by asking the students where and how they study. Ask for volunteers to talk about their strategies. List ideas on the chalkboard or chart tablet.

2. Distribute the *Study Skills Assessment* and give students a few minutes to complete it.

3. Display the *Study Skills and Habits* poster and present the following information:

   a. *Know your learning style.* Where and how do you study best? Do you like to work alone, with a friend, at the library, or at a desk in your room? Do you learn best by outlining, making mind maps, drawing diagrams, reading, acting things out, or talking over ideas with someone?

   b. *Study the difficult subjects first.* Harder assignments take more energy than easier ones, so save the "light" things for later.

   c. *Take short, frequent breaks during study sessions.* Whenever possible, study for approximately 20 minutes and then take a 5-minute break. You'll tend to remember better what you learn at the beginning and end of each study period, so create more beginnings and endings. Give your brain a break.

   d. *Set goals for your study time.* Decide ahead of time how far you plan to read, how many questions you will answer, or how many problems you will solve. Then stick to your goals.

   e. *Have a special study area.* Most students study best in a quiet place, away from the phone and the TV. Using a desk or a table is better than lying across your bed. Give your body the signal that it is time to study, not time to sleep.

   f. *Study effectively.* Look at headings and subheadings. Answer questions and read summaries at the ends of chapters. Write down important terms and vocabulary, as well as any questions you have. See how much information you can get from looking at graphs and diagrams. Read new information more slowly. Skim to review.

   g. *Study regularly.* Don't save everything until the last minute. Study often enough and for long enough periods to get your work done without "cramming." Cramming is stressful—physically and mentally.

   h. *Pretend you are a "paid" student.* If you were employed as a student, would you be earning your wages? If your breaks are longer than your study sessions, you would probably have your pay "docked" or lose your job.

4. Ask the students to choose at least one skill or strategy and commit to trying it over the weeks that the group meets.

Discussion

1. "What is meant by 'learning style'?"
2. "Why is it important to study in ways that are in keeping with your learning style? What happens if you don't?"
3. "How effective do you want your study habits to be?"
4. "What resources can help you accomplish that?"
5. "What will be better for you when you have implemented your study plan?"

Evaluation

Students will describe the best study systems for themselves and their plans to implement them.

---

* Also available on CD

Note. From *Group Activities for Counselors* (pp. 118–119), by S. Elliot, 1994, Austin, TX: PRO-ED, Inc. Copyright 1994 by PRO-ED, Inc. Adapted with permission.

Study Skills Assessment

Answer these questions about your study habits. Mark the answer that best describes you at this time.

		Always	Sometimes	Seldom	Never
1.	Do you know and use your best learning style?				
2.	Do you study the difficult subjects first?				
3.	Do you take short, frequent breaks during study sessions?				
4.	Do you set goals for your study time?				
5.	Do you have a special study area?				
6.	Do you read and study effectively?				
7.	Do you study regularly?				
8.	If you were a "paid" student, would you earn your wages?				

Note. From *Group Activities for Counselors* (p. 120), by S. Elliot, 1994, Austin, TX: PRO-ED, Inc. Copyright 1994 by PRO-ED, Inc. Adapted with permission.

Study Skills and Habits

1. Know your learning style.

2. Study the difficult subjects first.

3. Take short, frequent breaks during study sessions.

4. Set goals for your study time.

5. Have a special study area.

6. Study effectively.

7. Study regularly.

8. Pretend you are a "paid" student.

RESPONSIBLE BEHAVIOR

Note. From *Group Activities for Counselors* (pp. 118–119), by S. Elliot, 1994, Austin, TX: PRO-ED, Inc. Copyright 1994 by PRO-ED, Inc. Adapted with permission.

SOS! *A Practical Guide*

Freedom and Responsibility

Objectives

Group members will:

1. define what is responsible behavior in one situation, and

2. discuss the meaning of freedom and its relationship to responsibility.

Materials

Writing materials

192

Procedure

1. Read the following quotation to the group and discuss its meaning:

   Freedom is a partial, negative aspect of responsibility which is richer and more complete in meaning. We may become free from the immediate and yet remain irresponsible. We cannot become responsible, however, without also becoming free (p. 152). —John Wild, *Existence and the World of Freedom*

2. Tell the students that you are going to read them a brief story. (Alternative: Make copies of the story and have the group members take turns reading parts of it aloud.) The story will be followed by some thinking questions. Ask them to make notes as you read that relate to (a) who is responsible to whom; (b) what the individuals should do in order to behave responsibly; and (c) any specific question asked.

3. The Story: **Judy and the Orioles**

The Orioles girls' softball team has been practicing after school and winning most of its games. Judy is the best pitcher. The most important game of the season is coming up next weekend, which is a three-day holiday. This game will determine which of the teams make the finals. Everything is going fine until Judy tells her teammates that for months her parents have been planning a camping trip for that weekend, and they expect her to go with them. The members of the team become angry and upset. They try to convince Judy to stay and pitch, but she says she's free to do as she pleases.

Discussion

1. "Who is responsible for what? ... to whom?"

2. "Is Judy responsible to the team, to her parents, or to herself?"

3. "Are Judy's parents responsible to the team?"

4. "Is it the coach's responsibility to persuade Judy's parents to cancel the trip or allow Judy to stay?"

5. "Was it Judy's responsibility to check the schedule and see that her parents were informed?"

6. "How much freedom should Judy have in this situation to decide what to do?"

7. "Why is it important for people to understand to whom they are responsible?"

8. "When do we have the right to be responsible to ourselves?"

9. "What makes behavior responsible or irresponsible?"

10. "What role does culture play in how we view our responsibilities?"

Evaluation

Students will use their understanding of freedom and responsibility to make choices about behavior.

RESPONSIBLE BEHAVIOR

Note. From *50 Activities for Teaching Emotional Intelligence, Level III: High School* (p. 89), by D. Schilling and S. Palomares, 1999, Austin, TX: PRO-ED, Inc. Copyright 1999 by PRO-ED, Inc. Adapted with permission.

Who's in Charge?

Objective
Group members will recognize the degree of their personal control over events.

Materials
*Who's in Charge?** sheets

Procedure

1. Introduce the activity by asking students to indicate if they feel as though they have control over things that happen in their lives.
2. Distribute the *Who's in Charge?* sheet to each student. Have students read each situation and mark the degree of control they feel they have over it.

Discussion
1. "Share examples of any items you marked as being your fault only."
2. "Share examples of items you marked as being others' fault only."
3. "How much personal control do you think you have over what happens to you?"
4. "If you don't think you have much, what can you do about it?"
5. "How much control is desirable?"

Evaluation
Students indicate an understanding of their personal power in their lives as they attribute responsibility appropriately in real-life situations.

* Also available on CD

Note. From *Thinking, Feeling, Behaving, Grades 7–12* (pp. 17–18), by A. Vernon, 1989, Champaign, IL: Research Press. Copyright 1989 by Research Press. Adapted with permission.

RESPONSIBLE BEHAVIOR

Who's in Charge?

Read each of the situations and mark on the continuum to indicate the degree to which you feel you or others are in charge of what happens. There are three blanks at the end of the list to fill in with your own situations.

1. Others' fault totally ├----------------------------------┤ Your fault totally

   Failed a test

2. Others' fault totally ├----------------------------------┤ Your fault totally

   Didn't do an assignment

3. Others' fault totally ├----------------------------------┤ Your fault totally

   Didn't have enough money to buy a gift
   because you spent your allowance

4. Others' fault totally ├----------------------------------┤ Your fault totally

   Your group didn't learn their parts for the play

5. Others' fault totally ├----------------------------------┤ Your fault totally

   You got talked into TP-ing a neighbor's house

6. Others' fault totally ├----------------------------------┤ Your fault totally

   _____

7. Others' fault totally ├----------------------------------┤ Your fault totally

   _____

8. Others' fault totally ├----------------------------------┤ Your fault totally

   _____

Note. From *Thinking, Feeling, Behaving, Grades 7–12* (p. 18), by A. Vernon, 1989, Champaign, IL: Research Press. Copyright 1989 by Research Press. Adapted with permission.

RESPONSIBLE BEHAVIOR

The Turtle Technique for Tempering Anger

Objective

Group members will use a visualization technique to help them inhibit negative behavior when angry.

Materials

The Turtle Trick poster*; *1–2–3—Turtle!** poster; *Turtle Power!** sheets copied on green card stock or laminated; 6 brads for each student; scissors

Procedure

1. Start by talking to the students about anger as one of the emotions we all feel from time to time. Have students think about a time recently when they were angry. Say: *Since we know that anger is a feeling, we know that it's not bad to be angry. Anger is a very strong feeling that can give us the energy we need to solve problems. When we know how to control it, we can keep it from getting us into trouble. When we blow up and lose our tempers, we almost always cause trouble for ourselves. Think about a time when somebody did something that made you so mad you just exploded and then got into trouble for it. Since we all lose our tempers sometimes, what we need is a plan for what we are going to do when we feel ourselves getting angry so we don't blow up. Today, we're going to learn something called the Turtle Trick. The Turtle Trick is a clever way to calm yourself down when you get mad so that you don't do anything mean or get yourself in trouble.*

2. Show the students the *Turtle Trick* poster, point to the top picture and say: *This is how the turtle looks when it is not upset. Now what does the turtle do when someone bothers it?* Point to the bottom picture. *It goes into its shell. Then nobody can hurt it and it can't hurt anybody else.*

3. Display the *1–2–3—Turtle!* poster, covering Steps 1, 2, and 3 with a sheet of paper. Uncover each of the steps as you talk about it. *When someone says things that make you angry, you can go inside your shell, just like the turtle. Then, while you're inside your safe, warm shell, you can take some deep breaths and relax. While you're inside your shell you can calmly think of a good plan to solve the problem. This turtle decided he would just walk away.*

4. Distribute copies of *Turtle Power!* Have students cut out all of the parts and punch holes through the Xs. Assemble their turtles by aligning the holes and pushing brads through the holes.

5. Have students suggest situations in which they could become angry and lose their tempers. As each student talks about getting angry have the student use his or her turtle and practice the steps of (a) going inside the shell, (b) taking deep breaths and relaxing, and (c) thinking of a good plan to solve the problem.

CONFLICT RESOLUTION

Discussion

1. "Why is it a good idea to keep from losing our tempers when we get angry?"

2. "How will remembering to use *1–2–3—Turtle!* help you?"

3. "What will _____ say when you are able to use the Turtle Trick the next time you are angry?"

Evaluation

Students demonstrate the practice of staying calm when angry and making a plan to solve the problem.

CONFLICT RESOLUTION

---

* Also available on CD

Note. From *Helping Kids Handle Anger* (pp. 54, 63–69), by P. Huggins, 1998, Longmont, CO: Sopris West. Copyright 1998 by Sopris West. Adapted with permission.

The Turtle Trick

Here's how a turtle looks when it's not upset.

CONFLICT RESOLUTION

This is the turtle, safe in its shell.

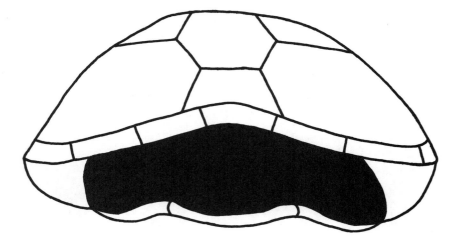

Note. From *Helping Kids Handle Anger* (p. 63), by P. Huggins, 1998, Longmont, CO: Sopris West. Copyright 1998 by Sopris West. Adapted with permission.

1–2–3—TURTLE!

When you are feeling ANGRY or UPSET:

1. Go inside your shell.

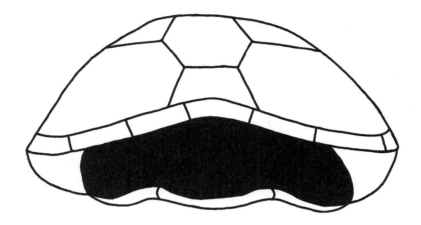

199

2. Take some deep breaths and relax.

3. Think of a good plan to solve the problem.

CONFLICT RESOLUTION

Note. From *Helping Kids Handle Anger* (p. 65), by P. Huggins, 1998, Longmont, CO: Sopris West. Copyright 1998 by Sopris West. Adapted with permission.

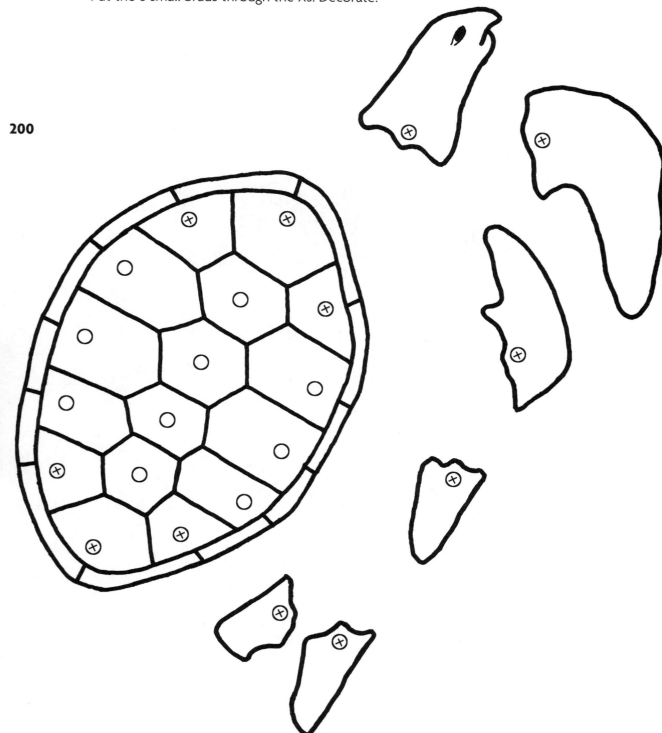

Turtle Power!

Cut out the turtle's shell, the turtle's head, and the turtle's legs. Match the pieces at the Xs. Put the 6 small brads through the Xs. Decorate!

Note. From *Helping Kids Handle Anger* (p. 67), by P. Huggins, 1998, Longmont, CO: Sopris West. Copyright 1998 by Sopris West. Adapted with permission.

Turtle Power!
(Continued)

201

Turtle OUT.

Turtle IN.

Note. From *Helping Kids Handle Anger* (p. 69), by P. Huggins, 1998, Longmont, CO: Sopris West. Copyright 1998 by Sopris West. Adapted with permission.

Using Refusal Skills

Objectives

Group members will:

1. learn effective methods for saying "no," and

2. practice refusal skills by role-playing actual situations.

Materials

Copies of *The Cool Kid's Guide To Saying "No"* sheets*; *Refusal* cards*

Procedure

1. Talk about the definition and goals of refusal skills. Refusal skills are ways of saying "no" skillfully. They put you in control of a situation. In the process, you think through the situation and make a conscious decision.

2. Distribute *The Cool Kid's Guide to Saying "No"* sheets. Read through the refusal skills with the students, answering questions and facilitating discussion.

3. Read one of the situations from the *Refusal* cards. Go through the refusal skills, one at a time, explaining how each skill could be used in the given situation.

4. Ask two students to role-play the situation in front of the group. Coach the students as needed.

5. Have the students take turns picking cards and have group members explain how each refusal skill could be used.

Discussion

1. "What is the hardest part about using refusal skills?"

2. "When you can keep from arguing and debating, how will things be better for you?"

3. "What kind of body language is important in situations like these?"

4. "How can you be sure that you will remember these steps when actually facing a situation?"

Evaluation

Students demonstrate effective use of refusal skills in real-life situations.

---

* Also available on CD

Note. From *Group Activities for Counselors* (pp. 79–82), by S. Elliot, 1994, Austin, TX: PRO-ED, Inc. Copyright 1994 by PRO-ED, Inc. Adapted with permission.

The Cool Kid's Guide to Saying "No"

What can you say when someone tries to get you to do something you don't want to do? How should you respond when someone asks you to take part in something that is illegal or dangerous?

Say "no" once. Say "no" twice. Say "no" again. Say "no" and leave. Here are some helpful guidelines:

203

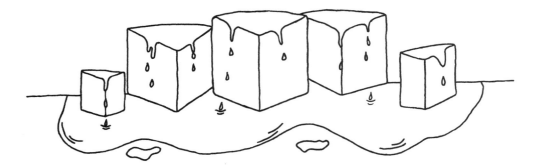

1. *Say "no."* Say it clearly, flatly, and confidently. Be assertive. When someone pressures you in a friendly way, remember that you can be friendly, too—even humorous—and be assertive at the same time.

2. *Say "no" and give a reason.* Briefly state why you are not going to do whatever the person is suggesting. Use appropriate voice and body language. Let your facial expression show calm confidence. Speak clearly, in a firm, steady voice.

3. *Say "no" and suggest something else to do.* There are lots of ways to have fun. Think of something you both enjoy that is safe and legal. Suggest it, but don't get into a debate.

4. *Say "no" and leave.* Don't waste time arguing with the person. If Steps 1–3 haven't worked, walk away. If you are threatened, skip Steps 1–3 and leave immediately.

Note. From *Group Activities for Counselors* (p. 82), by S. Elliot, 1994, Austin, TX: PRO-ED, Inc. Copyright 1994 by PRO-ED, Inc. Adapted with permission.

SOS! *A Practical Guide*

Refusal Cards

The person sitting next to you in the classroom has taken a pencil from another student at your table. He tells you to take one too. CR-P-2	At recess you played basketball and, after a close game, your team lost. Some of your teammates start booing the other team and want you to join them. CR-P-2
You are standing with a group of friends who start saying bad things about one of your other friends. They want you to say bad things too. CR-P-2	You and your friend borrowed a boy's video game and accidentally dropped it on the sidewalk. The case cracked. Your friend wants you to tell the boy that it was broken when you borrowed it. CR-P-2
Your brother wants you to go with him to a place your mother says is off limits. He says, "Come on. No one will know." CR-P-2	A friend wants you do something you know is wrong. She says, "If you were my friend, you would do this with me." CR-P-2
Two older kids at school tell you to do something that you know is dangerous. They say, "What ... are you chicken?" CR-P-2	Your cousin wants you to go some-place with her even though your aunt told you both to stay home. Your cousin says, "We won't get caught." CR-P-2
An older boy joins you and some other kids while you are playing in the neighborhood. He has some cigarettes that the other kids decide to smoke. He says, "I dare you." CR-P-2	A student in your class tells you to do his homework for him. He says, "No one will know." CR-P-2

204

Expressing Your Anger

Objective
Group members will express anger without hitting.

Materials
Copies of *Expressing Your Anger* sheets*; *Anger* cards*

Procedure
1. Talk about anger and the following points: feeling angry is okay; it's what we do with our anger that matters.

205

2. Model expressing anger by using the strategies on the *Expressing Your Anger* sheets:
   - Stop and count to 5
   - Why am I angry?
   - Choose: Tell a person, walk away, or take three deep breaths
   - Write about how I feel
   - Problem solve
3. Have students take turns selecting from the *Anger* cards and role-playing, using the steps to express their anger appropriately.

Discussion
1. "What is the hardest part about expressing anger?"
2. "When you can express anger without blowing up or hitting, how will things be better for you?"
3. "What kind of body language is important in situations like these?"
4. "How can you be sure that you will remember these steps when actually facing a situation?"

Evaluation
Students demonstrate effective expression of anger in real-life situations.

CONFLICT RESOLUTION

* Also available on CD

Note. From *Getting to Know You! Social Skills Curriculum for Grades 1–3* (pp. 190–191), by D. Hanken and J. Kennedy, 1998, Minneapolis, MN: Educational Media Corporation. Copyright 1998 by Educational Media Corporation. Adapted with permission.

SOS! *A Practical Guide*

Expressing Your Anger

1. Stop and count to 5.

2. Why am I angry?

3. Choose:

  A. Tell a person.

  B. Walk away.

  C. Take three deep breaths.

4. Write about how I feel.

5. Problem solve.

Note. From *Getting to Know You! Social Skills Curriculum for Grades 1–3* (p. 191), by D. Hanken and J. Kennedy, 1998, Minneapolis, MN: Educational Media Corporation. Copyright 1998 by Educational Media Corporation. Adapted with permission.

CONFLICT RESOLUTION

Anger Cards

Your friend talks about you
behind your back.

CR-P-3

Your teacher treats you unfairly.

CR-P-3

You get blamed for something
you didn't do.

CR-P-3

Your parents won't let you stay
overnight at a friend's house.

CR-P-3

You forgot your homework at
home and are angry at yourself.

CR-P-3

A classmate hits you with a
pencil while trying to toss it
to someone else.

CR-P-3

Your teacher makes you stay
in from recess to finish
your seatwork.

CR-P-3

You are watching a TV show and
your dad comes in and changes
the channel.

CR-P-3

Your friend said he or she would
play with you, but now he or she is
playing with someone else instead.

CR-P-3

Your group won't go along with
your ideas for the project you all
have been assigned.

CR-P-3

CONFLICT RESOLUTION

Note. From *Getting to Know You! Social Skills Curriculum for Grades 1–3* (pp. 190–191), by D. Hanken and J. Kennedy, 1998, Minneapolis, MN: Educational Media Corporation. Copyright 1998 by Educational Media Corporation. Adapted with permission.

Exploring Alternatives to Conflict

Objective
Group members will learn and practice specific strategies for resolving conflict.

Materials
Copies of *Conflict Resolution Strategies* sheets*

Procedure

208

1. Distribute the *Conflict Resolution Strategies* sheets. Explain to the students that in conflict situations, certain kinds of behaviors tend to help people solve their problems. As a group, read and discuss the strategies. Give examples, and ask the students to describe problems that might be resolved by each alternative.

2. Invite a member of the group to describe a conflict situation. Clarify the problem and then engage the group in speculating as to the appropriateness of each strategy in that situation. Ask the group to agree on a strategy to test. Have members of the group act out the conflict and its resolution, using the alternative chosen. At the conclusion of the role play, debrief the actors and discuss the effectiveness of the solution.

Discussion

1. "Why is it better to practice positive alternatives, rather than wait for conflict to occur and then try the alternatives?"

2. "Which strategies are hardest to use and why? Which are easiest? Which work best for you and why?"

3. "At what point do you think you should get help to resolve a conflict?"

Evaluation
Students demonstrate the effective use of several conflict resolution strategies in real-life situations.

CONFLICT RESOLUTION

---

* Also available on CD

Note. From *Group Activities for Counselors* (pp. 94–95), by S. Elliot, 1994, Austin, TX: PRO-ED, Inc. Copyright 1994 by PRO-ED, Inc. Adapted with permission.

Conflict Resolution Strategies

Have you ever been in a conflict? Of course! No matter how much you try to avoid them, conflicts happen. They are a part of life. What makes conflicts upsetting is not knowing how to handle them. If you don't know something helpful to do, you may end up making things worse. So, study these strategies, and the next time you see a conflict coming, try one!

1. *Share.*

   Whatever the conflict is about, keep (or use) some of it yourself, and let the other person have or use some.

2. *Take turns.*

   Use or do something for a little while. Then let the other person take a turn.

3. *Actively listen.*

   Let the other person talk while you listen carefully. Really try to understand the person's feelings and ideas.

4. *Postpone.*

   If you (or the other person) are very angry or tired, put off dealing with the conflict until another time.

5. *Use humor.*

   Look at the situation in a comical way. Don't take it too seriously.

6. *Compromise.*

   Offer to give up part of what you want and ask the other person to do the same.

7. *Express regret.*

   Say that you are sorry about the situation, *without* taking the blame.

8. *Problem solve.*

   Discuss the problem and try to find a solution that is acceptable to both you and the other person.

209

CONFLICT RESOLUTION

Note. From *Group Activities for Counselors* (p. 95), by S. Elliot, 1994, Austin, TX: PRO-ED, Inc. Copyright 1994 by PRO-ED, Inc. Adapted with permission.

SOS! *A Practical Guide*

Up and Down Escalators: Raising and Lowering the Level of Conflict

Objectives

Group members will:

1. identify behaviors that escalate and de-escalate conflict, and

2. practice using communication skills to control the escalation of conflicts.

Materials

Paper and black markers for each student; *Up and Down Escalators* scenarios* to be read to the group

Procedure

1. In your own words, introduce the concept of conflict escalation and de-escalation. For example, say:

   Imagine an escalator, such as the kind you use at the mall. An escalator moves people up and down from one level to another. The same is true with behaviors that escalate and de-escalate conflict. Some words or actions raise, or escalate, the conflict to higher levels; other behaviors lower, or de-escalate the conflict, to lower levels. In judging the effects of certain behaviors on conflict, try to picture whether the behavior is making the conflict go up or down.

2. Distribute paper and markers. Ask the students to draw a large, bold arrow on the paper. When they have finished, tell them you are going to read them two scenarios. As you read, they are to listen closely to the statements and actions of each character in the scenario. When they hear a statement or action that is likely to escalate the conflict, they should hold their arrows high, pointing up. When they hear a statement or action that is likely to de-escalate the conflict, they should hold their arrows pointing down.

3. Read each scenario slowly, allowing time for the students to respond. Notice if any of the behaviors draw mixed reactions from the students. After you have read each scenario, go back and role-play the parts that caused disagreement, with volunteers taking the two roles. Demonstrate and discuss how voice tone, facial expression, and body posture contribute greatly to determining whether a specific behavior is escalating or de-escalating.

Discussion

1. "What types of behaviors almost always escalate a conflict?"

2. "What types of behaviors have a good chance of de-escalating a conflict?"

3. "Do you think being aware of whether a conflict is escalating or de-escalating can help you control the conflict? How?"

4. "What have you learned from this activity that will make a difference in the way you handle conflict?"

210

CONFLICT RESOLUTION

Evaluation

Students identify escalating and de-escalating behaviors and have a plan for incorporating this knowledge into their conflict resolution strategies.

* Also available on CD

Note. From *50 Activities for Teaching Emotional Intelligence, Level II: Middle School* (pp. 136–137), by D. Schilling and S. Palomares, 1996, Austin, TX: PRO-ED, Inc. Copyright 1996 by PRO-ED, Inc. Adapted with permission.

I. Jake and Kim are supposed to be working together to solve a math problem. Jake takes the problem sheet and starts to write his solution on it.

Kim: "Here, let me have that. I think I know how to do this." (Slides the paper away from Jake and starts to write on it.)

Jake: "Hey, I was right in the middle of something. Give that back to me." (Reaches over, pulls the paper back, and continues writing.)

Kim: "You're not doing it right, dummy. You're going to have to erase the whole thing."

Jake: "I'll erase your face in a minute if you don't stop bugging me."

Kim: "We're supposed to be doing this together, and you're not listening to me!"

Jake: "Maybe I'd listen if you weren't so pushy. Anyway, I've finished it. There!"

Kim: "It's wrong. You can't prove your answer."

Jake: "Sure, I can."

Kim: "Show me, Mr. Smartie. You couldn't prove it if you worked all day. Ha ha ha." (Loudly.)

Jake: "Shut up, Kim. You always think you know everything, but you don't." (Pushes Kim away.)

II. Sergio and Tina are brother and sister. Sergio is watching TV. Tina walks in, picks up the remote control and changes the channel.

Sergio: "Why did you change the channel? I was watching that show!"

Tina: "I don't have time to argue with you. I have to watch this show for my science homework."

Sergio: "I don't care what it's for. That was my favorite show. Change it back right now!"

Tina: "You can't make me. I have just as much right to this TV as you do."

Sergio: "Not if I'm here first. I'm telling Mom!"

Tina: "Go ahead and tell Mom, crybaby. She'll just make you go do your homework."

Sergio: "I finished mine. What's the science program about?"

Tina: "Insects. Like you, creepy brother."

Note. From *50 Activities for Teaching Emotional Intelligence, Level II: Middle School* (p. 137), by D. Schilling and S. Palomares, 1996, Austin, TX: PRO-ED, Inc. Copyright 1996 by PRO-ED, Inc. Adapted with permission.

What Am I Thinking?

Objectives

Group members will:

1. identify how unclear communication can lead to conflict, and

2. describe ways in which communication can be made clear to prevent misunderstandings.

Materials

Six ft of yarn for each team of three; a pair of scissors for each team; 25 to 35 balloons of any shape or size in a variety of colors (not inflated) for each team; a thumbtack for each team; a set of *Inspector Instructions** for each team's inspector

213

Procedure

1. Divide the group into teams of about three people. Give each team a pair of scissors, 25 to 35 balloons, and about 6 ft of yarn. Choose one person from each team to be the inspector.

2. Take the inspectors aside and give them instructions privately. Tell the inspectors that their team will be handing them balloons. The balloons must be blown up, tied off, and have a piece of yarn tied around the stem. No two balloons of the same color may be handed to the inspector one right after the other. The same person may not hand two balloons to the inspector in a row. If you feel this may be too complicated for your inspectors to remember, have the instructions written down for them to refer to. Tell the inspectors they cannot answer any questions from their team. If you feel this set of rules is too hard for your group, take out the yarn-tying step. Don't make it too easy. The goal is for the team members to be frustrated.

3. Bring the inspectors back into the room. Explain to the team members that their assignment is to hand the balloons to their inspector in the correct manner. If the balloon is not handed to the inspector in the correct manner, the inspector will pop the balloon with his or her thumbtack. Each team has 25 to 35 balloons to hand the inspector. The inspector will place the "accepted" balloons on the floor to be counted at the end of the activity. The team with the most balloons accepted by the inspector is the winner. Explain that the inspector is not allowed to answer any questions. Give no further instructions except to clarify or repeat what you have already said. The object of the activity is to determine through trial and error the correct manner to hand a balloon to the inspector.

Discussion

1. "What was the correct manner to hand a balloon to the inspector?"

2. "How did you go about determining the correct manner?"

3. "How did you feel during the activity if you were the inspector?"

4. "How did you feel during the activity if you were one of the workers?"

5. "Have you ever had someone expect you to do something but not give you complete instructions? Explain."

6. "Have you ever had someone mad at you and when you asked what was wrong, that person tells you 'Nothing'?"

7. "How can we make our communication clear so misunderstandings don't happen?"

CONFLICT RESOLUTION

SOS! A Practical Guide

Evaluation

Students identify ways they can make their communication clearer and ways they can get clearer communication from others.

214

---

* Also available on CD

Note. From *More Activities That Teach* (pp. 326–328), by T. Jackson, 1995, Cedar City, UT: Red Rock Publishing. Copyright 1995 by Red Rock Publishing. Adapted with permission.

Inspector Instructions

How to Hand Off a Balloon

1. Balloons must be blown up.

2. Balloons must be tied off.

3. Balloons must have a piece of yarn tied around the stem.

4. No two balloons of the same color may be handed to the inspector one right after the other.

5. The same person may not hand two balloons in a row to the inspector.

CONFLICT RESOLUTION

Note. From *More Activities That Teach* (pp. 326–327), by T. Jackson, 1995, Cedar City, UT: Red Rock Publishing. Copyright 1995 by Red Rock Publishing. Adapted with permission.

Assessing Anger Styles

Objectives
Group members will:

1. identify two recent events that caused them to feel angry and describe what they did in each situation,

2. assess the effectiveness of their typical behaviors when angry,

3. examine and discuss several common anger styles, and

4. explain how they can choose more effective responses in situations that provoke anger.

Materials
Copies of *Assessing Your Anger* sheets*; *Anger Styles* poster*

Procedure

1. Share with the students: *Anger is a normal emotion. We all have characteristic ways of expressing anger. Let's call these "anger styles." Although anger styles are probably learned, they are deeply ingrained and therefore automatic—almost like reflexes. The results our anger styles produce have reinforced our tendency to repeat them over the years. Still, they may not be the most effective or productive behaviors to use in every situation. Learning to consciously choose how we express our anger will help us become better managers of conflict.*

2. Distribute the *Assessing Your Anger* sheets and ask the students to fill out the sheet.

3. Ask volunteers to tell the group what style they typically use to express their anger. Note which of their styles are on the *Anger Styles* poster, adding styles they mention that are not included.

4. Have students brainstorm the positive and negative outcomes that can occur as a result of using each style of anger on the poster.

Discussion

1. "How do we develop our styles of expressing anger?"

2. "Why do we persist in behaving in ways that don't work?"

3. "Under what circumstances would it be best to use stress-reduction techniques to deal with your anger, rather than confront the other person?"

4. "What skills do you need to have in order to assertively confront a situation or person and try to solve the problem that caused your anger?"

Evaluation
Students learn about their anger styles and the positive and negative consequences of using the various styles.

---

* Also available on CD

Note. From *50 Activities for Teaching Emotional Intelligence, Level III: High School* (pp. 126–129), by D. Schilling and S. Palomares, 1999, Austin, TX: PRO-ED, Inc. Copyright 1999 by PRO-ED, Inc. Adapted with permission.

Assessing Your Anger

Try to remember two recent incidents in which you became angry. Taking one incident at a time, think carefully about what happened and answer these questions as honestly as you can.

Anger Incident #1

What caused your anger?

How intense were your feelings?

Mildly Annoyed   **Furious**

217

How did your body feel?

What were your thoughts?

What did you feel like doing?

What did you do?

What was the result?

How effective was your behavior? Did it make matters a lot worse, or did it produce the results you wanted without hurting anyone?

Explain: _____

_____ .

Anger Incident #2

What caused your anger?

How intense were your feelings?

Mildly Annoyed   **Furious**

How did your body feel?

What were your thoughts?

What did you feel like doing?

What did you do?

What was the result?

How effective was your behavior? Did it make matters a lot worse, or did it produce the results you wanted without hurting anyone?

Explain: _____

_____ .

CONFLICT RESOLUTION

Note. From *50 Activities for Teaching Emotional Intelligence, Level III: High School* (pp. 128–129), by D. Schilling and S. Palomares, 1999, Austin, TX: PRO-ED, Inc. Copyright 1999 by PRO-ED, Inc. Adapted with permission.

SOS! *A Practical Guide*

Anger Styles

Anger Style	+	−
Blowing up or attacking		
Withdrawing or refusing to talk		
Suppressing, denying, or hiding feelings —pretending or being phony —use of alcohol or other drugs —overeating —excessive watching of TV		
Getting even —in hidden ways (passive–aggressive) —openly, through punishment		
Displacing feelings (taking them out on someone or something else)		
Releasing anger through stress reduction —exercise —tasks or chores that require physical activity —relaxation, music, or meditation —talking with a friend, parent, counselor, etc.		
Assertively confronting the situation —explaining the problem and your feelings —attacking the problem, *not* the person		

218

CONFLICT RESOLUTION

Note. From *50 Activities for Teaching Emotional Intelligence, Level III: High School* (p. 127), by D. Schilling and S. Palomares, 1999, Austin, TX: PRO-ED, Inc. Copyright 1999 by PRO-ED, Inc. Adapted with permission.

Problem Solving:
The Win–Win Strategy

Objectives
Group members will:

1. examine a win–win problem-solving process and discuss its benefits, and

2. practice using problem solving to resolve specific conflicts.

Materials

219

Copies of *Getting to Win–Win* sheets*; chalkboard

Procedure
1. Distribute copies of the *Getting to Win–Win* sheets and give the students a few minutes to read it. Ask for questions and facilitate a discussion of the benefits of problem solving. For example, you might say: *Of all of the strategies for resolving conflicts, problem solving is the most productive—the one most likely to leave both people feeling satisfied. By working together to develop the best possible solution, disputants:*

   - *interact in positive ways.*
   - *listen to each other's concerns.*
   - *combine their brain power to create alternative solutions.*
   - *choose a solution that allows both to feel they have "won."*

2. Have the students get together in pairs to practice the win–win process. Tell them to role-play a real conflict that one of the partners had experienced recently. Remind the person with the conflict to describe as accurately as possible both the circumstances of the conflict and the role of the other disputant before starting to role-play.

Discussion
1. "How did you feel as you worked together to resolve your conflict?"

2. "How satisfied are you with your solution? Explain."

3. "What are the hardest parts of the process? ... the easiest parts?"

4. "Problem solving doesn't work for every conflict. When do you think you would use this strategy?"

5. "What skills do you need to work on in order to improve your ability to handle conflict this way?"

Evaluation
Students learn about the win–win problem-solving strategy and practice it on real-life conflict situations they have experienced.

* Also available on CD

Note. From *Group Activities for Counselors* (pp. 96–98), by S. Elliot, 1994, Austin, TX: PRO-ED, Inc. Copyright 1994 by PRO-ED, Inc. Adapted with permission.

CONFLICT RESOLUTION

Getting to Win–Win

Have you ever had a conflict with one of your friends? If so, you know how easily conflict can damage a relationship. Sometimes it takes months to patch things up. Here's a way of handling conflict that can actually make a relationship stronger. By following these steps, you can make sure that both you and your friend end up feeling pretty good. Try it!

When you are in conflict:

1. Use an I-message to express your feelings and concerns.

2. Try to use a calm tone of voice and open, attentive body language.

3. Listen actively to the other person's side of the story. Don't interrupt. Try to understand his or her perceptions and feelings.

4. If you don't understand something, ask for more information. Say, "Could you tell me more about that ..." or "I don't think I understand. What exactly do you mean?"

5. Define the problem. After you have listened to each other's side of the story, work together to agree on exactly what the problem is. Include all parts of the problem in your definition.

6. Brainstorm possible solutions. You might want to write these down. Include all kinds of ideas, even ones that sound a little crazy.

7. Together, agree on the solution that has the best chance of solving the problem (the one you defined together). Combine several alternatives if necessary.

8. If no solution seems possible, put the problem on hold for a few days. Agree on a day and time to get together again. In the meantime, rethink the problem.

220

Note. From *Group Activities for Counselors* (p. 98), by S. Elliot, 1994, Austin, TX: PRO-ED, Inc. Copyright 1994 by PRO-ED, Inc. Adapted with permission.

CONFLICT RESOLUTION

Managing Moods

Objectives

Group members will:

1. explain how moods are affected by feelings left over from conflicts,

2. identify problems and feelings associated with specific conflicts, and

3. describe strategies for releasing residual feelings and managing negative moods.

Materials

Copies of *Lousy Moods* cards*; chalkboard or chart paper; 3" × 5" index cards   **221**

Procedure

1. Have a student draw from the *Lousy Moods* cards and read the scenario aloud. Ask the discussion questions for each scenario. Continue through at least two more cards.

2. Help the students recognize and describe how Ahmad, Rita, Mike, and Jeremy each started with a specific problem or conflict that produced certain feelings (frustration, worry, disappointment, anxiety, embarrassment, etc.). In all four cases, these first feelings were followed by anger, and the anger carried over into unrelated activities involving unsuspecting friends.

3. Write the following guidelines on the board or chart paper:

   Guide to Managing Moods

   • BUY YOURSELF SOME TIME!!!!

   • Fill in this time with mood management strategies.

   • It takes time for feelings to go away naturally. Don't let them affect other activities.

4. Have the students discuss why it is so important to "buy time" when you are experiencing negative feelings associated with a problem or conflict.

5. On the board or chart paper, write the heading, "Mood Management Strategies." Ask the students to help you brainstorm positive, healthy ways of releasing anger and other negative feelings. List all ideas. Include items such as:

   • Talk with a trusted friend.

   • Run laps around the block or track.

   • Leave the situation and take several slow, deep breaths.

   • Get something to eat or drink.

   • Listen to relaxing music.

   • Take a walk in a pleasant, natural setting.

   • Imagine being in a favorite place.

   • Work on a project or hobby.

6. Give each student a 3" × 5" card. Suggest that students write down three or four mood management ideas that they think might work for them. Encourage them to carry the card with them, or tape it to a mirror or closet door at home as a reminder.

SOS! A Practical Guide

CONFLICT RESOLUTION

Discussion

1. "What was the *real* problem in the scenarios?"
2. "What were the first feelings about the problem?"
3. "What are some of the other feelings?"
4. "What did the angry person do that caused the other person to behave the way he or she did?"
5. "Why did the angry person respond as he or she did?"

Evaluation

Students learn about how their moods are affected by instances when they feel anger. Students make a plan to keep negative feelings from flowing into other relationships with other people.

222

* Also available on CD

Note. From *50 Activities for Teaching Emotional Intelligence, Level III: High School* (pp. 45–47), by D. Schilling and S. Palomares, 1999, Austin, TX: PRO-ED, Inc. Copyright 1999 by PRO-ED, Inc. Adapted with permission.

CONFLICT RESOLUTION

Lousy Moods Cards

Ahmad was just finishing a report on the computer when he hit the wrong key and erased all of his work. He felt totally frustrated and was starting to get angry with himself, but he had to get to his next class. Ahmad walked out of the computer room and down the hall. Lost in his thoughts about doing something so stupid, he stumbled right into Judy, knocking her books all over the floor. He gave her a disgusted look and yelled, "Why don't you look where you're going?"

CR-S-3

Rita was ready to leave for school, but she couldn't find her books and nobody seemed to know where they were. She had two assignments due that day and both were inside her books. She started to get upset. After nearly 30 minutes of searching, Rita found the books in one of her little sister's, Martha's, favorite hiding places. When she confronted her, Martha admitted hiding them. Even though she found her books, Rita was still mad at her sister and left for school late and in a terrible mood. When she walked into her first class, her best friend, Alexa, said, "Hi, girl. You look upset." Rita snapped, "Leave me alone. I don't want to talk to you!"

CR-S-3

Mike just found out that he didn't make the final cut for the basketball team. As he walked away from the gym, he started feeling angry. Mike thought it was unfair that some of the guys who did make the team couldn't shoot or maneuver nearly as well as he could. He felt crummy. When he walked around the corner, Mike saw a bunch of his friends talking. When Charlie saw Mike, he said, "What are you looking so down about?" Mike was embarrassed. He didn't want anyone to know he'd been cut, so all he said was, "None of your business," and walked off.

CR-S-3

Jeremy and Lea had been talking to each other for some time on the phone at night and at school. Jeremy was beginning to think that Lea really liked him. As he came out of school late one afternoon, he saw her sitting in a car talking to Tim. Jeremy started to get upset but he needed to get home for dinner. When he came through the door, his mother said, "Why don't you invite that nice Lea over for dinner sometime?" Jeremy threw his backpack in the corner and stomped out of the room.

CR-S-3

223

CONFLICT RESOLUTION

Note. From *50 Activities for Teaching Emotional Intelligence, Level III: High School* (p. 47), by D. Schilling and S. Palomares, 1999, Austin, TX: PRO-ED, Inc. Copyright 1999 by PRO-ED, Inc. Adapted with permission.

Consequences of Choices and Decisions

Objective
Group members will learn that there are consequences for poor choices and poor decisions.

Materials
Egg; bowl; glass of water; marker; *Consequences of Choices and Decisions* poster; *Problem* cards*

Procedure
1. Demonstrate cause-and-effect relationships by breaking an egg in a bowl or tipping a glass of water over.
2. Use the *Consequences of Choices and Decisions* poster to model for the group the strategies for making a decision after considering its consequences: (a) What are my choices? (b) What are the likely consequences of each choice? (c) Pick the best choice.
3. Use the *Problem* cards to brainstorm possibilities of choices and consequences.

Discussion
1. "What is cause and effect?"
2. "How will you plan to remember these steps when you face a decision?"

Evaluation
Students demonstrate considering consequences of decisions related to typical everyday decisions.

* Also available on CD

Note. From *Getting to Know You! Social Skills Curriculum for Grades 1–3* (pp. 163–165), by D. Hanken and J. Kennedy, 1998, Minneapolis, MN: Educational Media Corporation. Copyright 1998 by Educational Media Corporation. Adapted with permission.

224

DECISION MAKING

Consequences of Choices and Decisions

1. What are my choices?

2. What are the likely consequences of each choice?

3. Pick the best choice.

225

Note. From *Getting to Know You! Social Skills Curriculum for Grades 1–3* (p. 165), by D. Hanken and J. Kennedy, 1998, Minneapolis, MN: Educational Media Corporation. Copyright 1998 by Educational Media Corporation. Adapted with permission.

Problem Cards

226

Cause: Someone calls you a name.

DM-P-1

Cause: You disobey the playground supervisor.

DM-P-1

Cause: Someone shares his or her dessert with you.

DM-P-1

Cause: You give someone a compliment.

DM-P-1

Cause: Someone drinks too much soda.

DM-P-1

Cause: Someone writes on the bathroom wall with a marker.

DM-P-1

Cause: Someone starts a fire by playing with matches.

DM-P-1

Cause: You help fold the laundry.

DM-P-1

Cause: You make your bed without being told.

DM-P-1

Cause: You forgot to feed your pets.

DM-P-1

DECISION MAKING

(continues)

Problem Cards
(Continued)

Cause: You go outside in the rain
without a coat.

DM-P-1

Cause: You wake up late
on a school day.

DM-P-1

227

Cause: You forget your
homework at home.

DM-P-1

Cause: You aren't watching
the time and get home late
from a friend's house.

DM-P-1

Cause: Someone pushes you
in the lunch line.

DM-P-1

Cause: Someone draws
on your desk.

DM-P-1

Cause: You forget your lunch
money at home.

DM-P-1

Cause: You don't do your
homework, and it's due today.

DM-P-1

Cause: You tell your parents a lie.

DM-P-1

Cause: You introduce a new
student to your friends.

DM-P-1

DECISION MAKING

Note. From *Getting to Know You! Social Skills Curriculum for Grades 1–3* (p. 164), by D. Hanken and J. Kennedy, 1998, Minneapolis, MN: Educational Media Corporation. Copyright 1998 by Educational Media Corporation. Adapted with permission.

Goal Wheel

Objective
Group members will identify an individual goal and describe what they will do each day during the week to reach that goal.

Materials
Goal Wheel*

Procedure
228

1. Begin by talking to the students about what a goal is and how setting goals for ourselves helps us. Talk about how we work toward the achievement of goals over time. Model the selection of a short-term goal to be achieved over the next week. Have the students select a goal they would like to achieve during the week between group sessions.

2. Distribute the *Goal Wheels.* Have the students illustrate their goal and write the words to describe the goal in the center of the wheel.

3. In the space for each day on the wheel, students should use words or drawings to show steps to achieve goal attainment.

Discussion
1. "How will your life be better when you achieve your goal?"
2. "What will help you get to your goal?"
3. "What has helped you before when you were able to achieve a goal?"

Evaluation
Students demonstrate establishing a goal and deciding on the steps to reach it.

* Also available on CD

Note. From *Esteem Builders* (p. 257), by M. Borba, 1989, Austin, TX: PRO-ED, Inc. Copyright 1989 by PRO-ED, Inc. Adapted with permission.

DECISION MAKING

Goal Wheel

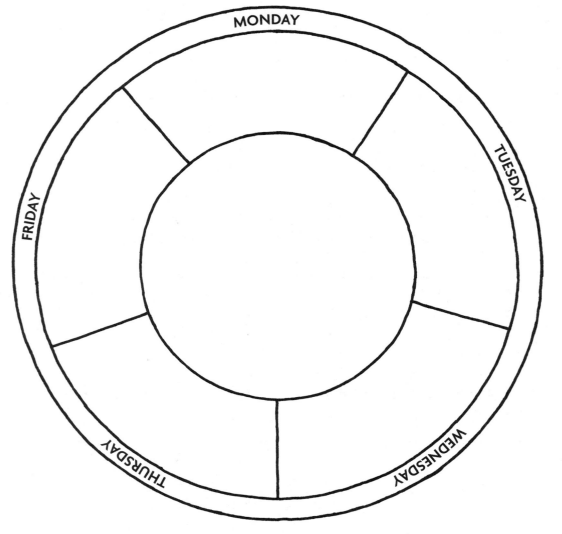

229

A picture of me making my goal:

DECISION MAKING

Note. From *Esteem Builders* (p. 257), by M. Borba, 1989, Austin, TX: PRO-ED, Inc. Copyright 1989 by PRO-ED, Inc. Adapted with permission.

Overcoming Obstacles to Goals

Objectives
Group members will:

1. identify a goal,
2. describe possible obstacles to reaching the goal, and
3. make a plan to overcome the obstacles.

Materials

230

*Climbing High Contract**

Procedure
1. Begin by talking to the students about obstacles to the goals we set. Tell students that when we think ahead to potential obstacles that may block us from reaching our goals, we can prepare for the obstacles and not let them overwhelm us.
2. Using the goal each student is working on, talk about instances in which students have encountered obstacles.
3. Follow these questions as you help each student identify the obstacles to his or her goals:
   - *Reaffirm your goal for yourself. What do you want to aim for?*
   - *What are the red flags that may stop you from reaching your goal?*
   - *What can you do to overcome these red flags?*
4. Distribute the *Climbing High Contract.* Have students complete the contract and then share their plans with the group.

Discussion
1. "How will your life be better when you achieve your goal?"
2. "What will help you get to your goal?"
3. "What has helped you before when you were able to achieve a goal?"

Evaluation
Students demonstrate establishing a goal and deciding on the steps to reach it.

DECISION MAKING

* Also available on CD

Note. From *Esteem Builders* (p. 253), by M. Borba, 1989, Austin, TX: PRO-ED, Inc. Copyright 1989 by PRO-ED, Inc. Adapted with permission.

Climbing High Contract

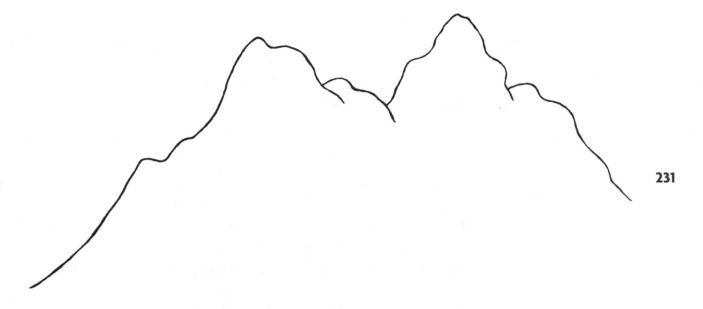

231

My goal is: _____ .

Steps I need to do to get there: _____

_____ .

Who or what I need to help me: _____

_____ .

I will try to make my goal by _____ .
 (date)

DECISION MAKING

Note. From *Esteem Builders* (p. 253), by M. Borba, 1989, Austin, TX: PRO-ED, Inc. Copyright 1989 by PRO-ED, Inc. Adapted with permission.

Decisions, Decisions!

Objectives
Group members will:

1. understand and describe how decisions are influenced by various factors, and

2. develop and practice a process for effective decision making.

Materials
Decision-Making Process poster*; *Decision-Making Process* cards*

Procedure
1. Review the *Decision-Making Process* poster with the students, examining each step and getting input from the students about how each step can be accomplished.

Step 1. Recognize and define the decision to be made.

Step 2. Know what is important to you (your values) and what you want to accomplish (your goal).

Knowing what is important to you and what you want to accomplish involves such things as likes, dislikes, values, and interests. Most important, it involves having goals.

Step 3. Study the information you have already; obtain and study new information, too.
You can get information by talking to people, visiting places, watching TV, and reading. Once you have the information, you must be able to evaluate it. If two people tell you to do opposite things, how are you going to know which is right? What if neither is right?

Step 4. List all of your alternatives.

Look into the future. Ask yourself what would be the probable outcome if you chose each of the alternatives available? For example, what would happen if

- *you did not go to college?*
- *you never got married?*
- *you dropped out of school?*
- *you decided to experiment with drugs?*
- *you became a professional rock singer?*
- *you decided never to drink alcohol?*
- *you decided not to have children?*

How did you make your predictions? What information did you use?

Step 5. List the advantages and disadvantages of each alternative.

Step 6. Make a decision.

When you reach the decision point, don't procrastinate. If you've done a good job on the other steps, you can choose the best alternative with confidence. Remember, if you don't choose, someone else may choose for you.

DECISION MAKING

Step 7. Develop a plan for carrying out your decision.

> *Not every decision requires an action plan, but the big ones usually do. The decision to attend a 4-year college in another state won't come true unless you make it. And that means more decisions. Can you think of what they might be?*

2. Ask the students to suggest a decision they might face. Go through the process, using the *Decision Cards* and having each student draw a card and respond in the order of the process to recommend a decision.

Discussion
1. "What did you learn about decision making from this activity?"
2. "Why is it important to know your interests and values when making decisions?"
3. "How can having goals help you make decisions?"

Evaluation
Students demonstrate the ability to follow the decision-making process and apply it to a decision in their lives.

---

* Also available on CD

Note. From *Activities for Counseling Underachievers* (pp. 75–79), by J. Bleuer, S. Palomares, and G. Walz, 1993, Austin, TX: PRO-ED, Inc. Copyright 1993 by PRO-ED, Inc. Adapted with permission.

© 2007 by PRO-ED, Inc.

SOS! *A Practical Guide*

The Decision-Making Process

Here are some steps to follow when you have a decision to make:

1. Recognize and define the decision to be made.

2. Know what is important to you (your values) and what you want to accomplish (your goal).

3. Study the information you have "already; obtain and study new information, too.

4. List all of your alternatives.

5. List the advantages and disadvantages of each alternative.

6. Make a decision.

7. Develop a plan for carrying out your decision.

234

Note. From *Activities for Counseling Underachievers* (p. 78), by J. Bleuer, S. Palomares, and G. Walz, 1993, Austin, TX: PRO-ED, Inc. Copyright 1993 by PRO-ED, Inc. Adapted with permission.

DECISION MAKING

The Decision-Making Process Cards

1. Recognize and define the decision to be made.

   DM-I-1

2. Know what is important to you (your values) and what you want to accomplish (your goal).

   DM-I-1

3. Study the information you have already; obtain and study new information, too.

   DM-I-1

4. List all of your alternatives.

   DM-I-1

5. List the advantages and disadvantages of each alternative.

   DM-I-1

6. Make a decision.

   DM-I-1

7. Develop a plan for carrying out your decision.

   DM-I-1

235

DECISION MAKING

Note. From *Activities for Counseling Underachievers* (p. 78), by J. Bleuer, S. Palomares, and G. Walz, 1993, Austin, TX: PRO-ED, Inc. Copyright 1993 by PRO-ED, Inc. Adapted with permission.

Setting and Attaining Goals

Objectives
Group members will:

1. explain that having a goal is the first step to achieving what one wants,
2. identify specific steps for attaining goals,
3. develop skills in setting practical and achievable goals, and
4. experience goal attainment.

Materials
Tips for Setting Goals* sheets; *Goal Achievement Score Sheets**

Procedure
1. This is a continuing activity, designed to be used with students over the course of the group sessions. This activity will allow them to build on and reinforce the goals they have identified to work on in the SOS group.
2. Remind the students that they have set goals for weekly work in group. This is an opportunity to document their progress on paper.
3. Distribute the *Tips for Setting Goals** sheets and the *Goal Achievement Score Sheets*. Take this time to remind students of the characteristics of good goals.
4. Allow group members to ask for help from the group, if needed, to word their goals.

Discussion
1. "How do you feel about having completed steps toward your goal?"
2. "What will help you get to your goal?"
3. "What has helped you before when you were able to achieve a goal?"

Evaluation
Students demonstrate the ability to establish a goal and decide on the steps to reach it.

236

DECISION MAKING

* Also available on CD

Note. From *Group Activities for Counselors* (pp. 123–127), by S. Elliot, 1994, Austin, TX: PRO-ED, Inc. Copyright 1994 by PRO-ED, Inc. Adapted with permission.

Tips for Setting Goals

1. *Goals must be clear and describe exactly what you want or will do.*

2. *Goals must be personal.* They must be about you, not someone else.

3. *Goals must be measurable.* You need to know when you have achieved your goal.

4. *Goals must have realistic time limits.*

5. *Goals must be manageable.* Divide big goals into several smaller, attainable goals or tasks. This will enable you to experience results in a shorter period of time.

6. *Goals must be stated in positive rather than negative terms.* (*I will do something* rather than *I won't do something.*)

7. *Goals must be written down.* People are more likely to achieve goals that are in writing. Written goals can be reviewed regularly, and they have more power. Like a contract with yourself, they are harder to neglect or forget.

Note. From *Group Activities for Counselors* (p. 127), by S. Elliot, 1994, Austin, TX: PRO-ED, Inc. Copyright 1994 by PRO-ED, Inc. Adapted with permission.

DECISION MAKING

Goal Achievement Score Sheet

GOAL #1 Steps Toward Achieving My Goal:	Review Date	Step Achieved	Step Not Achieved
1.			
2.			
3.			
4.			

GOAL #2 Steps Toward Achieving My Goal:	Review Date	Step Achieved	Step Not Achieved
1.			
2.			
3.			
4.			

GOAL #3 Steps Toward Achieving My Goal:	Review Date	Step Achieved	Step Not Achieved
1.			
2.			
3.			
4.			

238

DECISION MAKING

Note. From *Group Activities for Counselors* (p. 126), by S. Elliot, 1994, Austin, TX: PRO-ED, Inc. Copyright 1994 by PRO-ED, Inc. Adapted with permission.

Decisions and Outcomes

Objectives
Group members will:

1. understand and describe how decisions are influenced by many factors, and
2. state the outcomes and possible consequences of specific decisions.

Materials
More About Decisions sheets; *Decision Discussion* cards*; chart paper or chalkboard

239

Procedure
1. Begin by defining "decision making" as a process in which a person selects from two or more choices. Point out that:
   - A decision is not necessary unless there is more than one course of action to consider.
   - Not deciding is making a decision.
   - Two people facing similar decisions create unique outcomes because they want different things.
   - Learning decision-making skills increases the possibility that people can have what they want.
   - Each decision is limited by what people are able to do and what they are willing to do. Ability is increased by having more alternatives. Willingness is usually determined by values and goals.
2. Distribute the *More About Decisions* sheet and give students a few minutes to complete the sheet.
3. Use the *Decision Discussion* cards to prompt group discussion about experiences students have had with making decisions.

Discussion
1. "What did you find out about your 'worst decision' from this activity?"
2. "What is the difference between decisions and outcomes?"
3. "If your decision was truly bad, how could you have made a better one?"
4. "What kinds of decisions require study and thought?"

Evaluation
Students demonstrate how decisions are influenced and how outcomes can vary.

DECISION MAKING

---

* Also available on CD

Note. From *50 Activities for Teaching Emotional Intelligence, Level III: High School* (pp. 56–58), by D. Schilling and S. Palomares, 1999, Austin, TX: PRO-ED, Inc. Copyright 1999 by PRO-ED, Inc. Adapted with permission.

More About Decisions

Write down all of the decisions that you can remember making so far today.

Decisions

_____ 1. _____

_____ 2. _____

_____ 3. _____

_____ 4. _____

_____ 5. _____

_____ 6. _____

_____ 7. _____

_____ 8. _____

_____ 9. _____

Now go back through your list of decisions and code each one with a number from this scale:

0 = *I have no control over this type of decision; it is dictated by others.*
1 = *This type of decision is automatic, routine, or habitual.*
2 = *I occasionally think about this type of decision.*
3 = *I think about this type of decision, but I don't study it.*
4 = *I study this type of decision somewhat.*
5 = *I study this type of decision a lot.*

What does this exercise tell you about how you make most of your decisions?

_____

_____

240

DECISION MAKING

What is the worst decision you ever made? Write a brief description of it:

_____

_____

_____

_____

Decision or Outcome? Next time you're tempted to kick yourself over a "bad" decision, consider these points:

- When you say a decision is poor, you probably mean that the result or outcome is not what you wanted.
- Good decision making minimizes the possibility of getting bad outcomes, but it doesn't eliminate the possibility.
- A decision is the act of choosing among several possibilities, based on your judgments.
- An outcome is the result, consequence, or aftermath of the decision.
- You have direct control over the decision, but not over the outcome.
- A good decision does not guarantee a good outcome, but it does increase the chances of a good outcome.

Go back and look at your "worst" decision again. Was it really a bad decision, or was it a reasonable decision with a bad outcome?

DECISION MAKING

Note. From *50 Activities for Teaching Emotional Intelligence, Level III: High School* (p. 58), by D. Schilling and S. Palomares, 1999, Austin, TX: PRO-ED, Inc. Copyright 1999 by PRO-ED, Inc. Adapted with permission.

242

A Time I Had to Choose
the Best of Two Bad Things

DM-I-3

A Time I Had a Problem
and I Solved It

DM-I-3

A Time I Didn't Want
to Make a Decision

DM-I-3

A Time I Thought Over My
Decision and I Stuck to It

DM-I-3

A Time I Shared in
Making a Decision

DM-I-3

A Time I Used Good Judgment

DM-I-3

A Time I Thought It Over
and Then Decided

DM-I-3

Looking Back on a Decision I Made

DM-I-3

A Time I Had Trouble Deciding
the Right Thing to Do

DM-I-3

A Time I Had to Remake
My Decision

DM-I-3

DECISION MAKING

(continues)

Decision Discussion
(Continued)

A Time I Put Off Making a Decision DM-I-3	A Decision I Lived to Regret DM-I-3
It Was My Decision, But Someone Else Made It DM-I-3	The Hardest Decision I've Ever Made DM-I-3
One of the Best Decisions I've Ever Made DM-I-3	A Time I Made a Good Decision But Got a Poor Result DM-I-3
The Hardest Thing About Making Decisions Is ... DM-I-3	The Easiest Thing About Making Decisions Is ... DM-I-3
What It Takes To Be Decisive DM-I-3	A Time I Was Sure I Was Doing the Right Thing DM-I-3

DECISION MAKING

Note. From *50 Activities for Teaching Emotional Intelligence, Level III: High School* (p. 62), by D. Schilling and S. Palomares, 1999, Austin, TX: PRO-ED, Inc. Copyright 1999 by PRO-ED, Inc. Adapted with permission.

Decisions, Decisions!

Objectives

Group members will:

1. understand and describe how decisions are influenced by many factors, and

2. develop and practice a process for effective decision making.

Materials

The Decision-Making Process* sheets; chart paper or chalkboard

Procedure

1. Distribute the *Decision-Making Process* sheets. Read through the seven steps with the students, examining each one.

2. Ask for volunteers to share alternatives and their advantages and disadvantages.

3. Have students suggest a hypothetical decision that needs to be made. Have the students select one of the cards listing steps of the process. As you work through the process as a group, have each student talk about his or her step in the process.

Discussion

1. "How can this process improve your decision making?"

2. "Why is it important to take the time to think of alternatives?"

3. "How can having a goal make decisions simpler to make?"

Evaluation

Students demonstrate the ability to follow a decision-making process by applying it to real decisions they face in their lives.

---

* Also available on CD

Note. From *50 Activities for Teaching Emotional Intelligence, Level III: High School* (pp. 52–54), by D. Schilling and S. Palomares, 1999, Austin, TX: PRO-ED, Inc. Copyright 1999 by PRO-ED, Inc. Adapted with permission.

The Decision-Making Process

Here are some steps to follow when you have a decision to make:

1. Recognize and define the decision to be made.
2. Know what is important to you (your values) and what you want to accomplish (your goal).
3. Study the information you have already; obtain and study new information, too.
4. List all of your alternatives.
5. List the advantages and disadvantages of each alternative.
6. Make a decision.
7. Develop a plan for carrying out your decision.

245

Now let's see how the process really works. Think of a decision that you need to make in the next month. Define it here:

What is your goal relative to this decision?

What kinds of things that are important in your life (your values) might affect, or be affected by, this decision?

What kinds of information do you have or need?

Things to think about: Things to read:

People to talk to: Things to do:

What are your alternatives and what are the advantages and disadvantages of each?

Alternative #1:

Advantages: Disadvantages:

Alternative #2:

Advantages: Disadvantages:

Decision Point!
Which alternative has the best chance for producing the outcome you want?

Note. From *50 Activities for Teaching Emotional Intelligence, Level III: High School* (p. 53), by D. Schilling and S. Palomares, 1999, Austin, TX: PRO-ED, Inc. Copyright by 1999 PRO-ED, Inc. Adapted with permission.

DECISION MAKING

Approval and Consequences

Objective
Group members will recognize the advantages and disadvantages of doing something to gain social approval.

Materials
*Approval and Consequences** cards; magazine pictures of people drinking beer, kissing, fighting, smoking, etc.; chalkboard or chart paper

Procedure
1. Hold up the magazine pictures and ask students to describe what they see happening. Indicate that sometimes people do these things because they want to, but other times they do them because they want to be accepted by others. Ask students to pair up and think of other examples of things that could be done to get others' approval. List examples on the chalkboard.

2. Discuss the difference between doing something because you feel it is right for you, and doing something that doesn't feel right because you want the crowd's approval. Discuss the concept of consequences of doing things for peer approval, using the following example:

 Tony is a good student, but the kids he runs around with think doing homework and being smart are for nerds. So Tony stops studying and gets bad grades so he'll fit in.

3. Have students select from the *Approval and Consequences* cards, one at a time. Decide whether you want all students or only one student to respond to each card.

Discussion
1. "What are some of the consequences that have to be considered when deciding whether or not to do something?"
2. "What happens if you go against the crowd and do what you think is right for you?"
3. "When you are confronted with a conflict of this type, what process do you go through in deciding what to do?"
4. "If you go with the crowd but against what you think might be right for you, how do you feel?"
5. "What have you learned from this activity that you could apply to future conflict situations involving peer approval?"

Evaluation
Students demonstrate the ability to follow a decision-making process by applying it to real decisions they face in their lives.

---

* Also available on CD

Note. From *Thinking, Feeling, Behaving, Grades 7–12* (pp. 79–81), by A. Vernon, 1989, Champaign, IL: Research Press. Copyright 1989 by Research Press. Adapted with permission.

DECISION MAKING

Approval and Consequences

Chad and Tom are going to a movie. Next to the theater is a video arcade. Because they have a few minutes before the movie starts, they go inside. They see some kids from their school who invite them to come out to the parking lot and have a few beers. What could happen if Chad and Tom go? What could happen if they don't go?

DM-S-2

Marcia and Tim have been going out for about a month. Tim calls Marcia and tells her that his parents are gone for the night and he wants her to come over. Tim is older and has been urging Marcia not to be so uptight about making out with him. Marcia really likes Tim but can't decide what to do. What could happen if Marcia does go? What could happen if she doesn't go?

DM-S-2

Jenny and Sarah have been friends for a long time, but lately Jenny has been hanging around with a different crowd and hasn't called Sarah much. However, Jenny finally calls and asks Sarah to a party Friday night. Sarah goes to the party, but when she gets there, she notices that lots of kids are smoking pot. Jenny urges Sarah to try it, saying that it won't hurt anything. What could happen if Sarah does try it? What could happen if she doesn't try it?

DM-S-2

Tonya is really smart. Ever since she was in grade school, she has wanted to be a doctor. When her friends call her and want her to do things and she says she has to study, they make fun of her. She gets tired of having her friends call her a nerd and a bookworm all the time. She thinks that she might be losing her friends. What could happen if Tonya continues to study? What could happen if she doesn't continue to study?

DM-S-2

DECISION MAKING

Note. From *Thinking, Feeling, Behaving, Grades 7–12* (p. 81), by A. Vernon, 1989, Champaign, IL: Research Press. Copyright 1989 by Research Press. Adapted with permission.

Looking Back on a Decision I Made

Objective
Group members will describe and evaluate decisions they have made.

Materials
*Decisions** cards

Procedure

1. Say to the students, *Our topic for this session is "Looking Back on a Decision I Made." It's usually very easy for us to look back on something and see how we could have done it differently. That's called hindsight. Perhaps you made a decision once that you wouldn't make again today, or maybe, looking back, you feel proud of yourself for making the decision. Whatever the decision was, and whether or not you think it was a good decision now, if you would like to tell us about it, we would like to hear your story.*

2. Have students draw from the stack of *Decisions* cards and respond from their experience. Students may respond to one card each or have a go-around on each topic.

Discussion

1. "How did you feel about your decision when you made it? How do you feel about it now?"

2. "Which decisions were made after gathering facts and thinking things over?"

3. "Which decisions were the results of intuition, hunches, or just 'knowing'?"

Evaluation
Students demonstrate the ability to evaluate the decisions they have made and draw conclusions about how to make a decision they will be able to support afterward.

248

DECISION MAKING

* Also available on CD

Note. From *50 Activities for Teaching Emotional Intelligence, Level III: High School* (pp. 61–62), by D. Schilling and S. Palomares, 1999, Austin, TX: PRO-ED, Inc. Copyright 1999 by PRO-ED, Inc. Adapted with permission.

Decisions

A Time I Had to Choose the Better of Two Bad Things

DM-S-3

A Time I Had to Decide Between My Friend's Preference and Mine

DM-S-3

A Time I Didn't Want to Make a Decision Because I Knew People Would Not Approve

DM-S-3

A Time I Thought Over My Decision, and I Stuck to It

DM-S-3

A Time I Shared in Making a Decision

DM-S-3

A Time I Used Good Judgment

DM-S-3

A Time I Thought It Over and Then Decided

DM-S-3

Looking Back on a Decision I Made

DM-S-3

DECISION MAKING

A Time I Had Trouble Deciding the Right Thing to Do

DM-S-3

A Time I Had to Remake My Decision

DM-S-3

(continues)

SOS! A Practical Guide

Decisions
(Continued)

250

A Time I Put Off Making a Decision DM-S-3	A Decision I Lived to Regret DM-S-3
It Was My Decision, But Someone Else Made It DM-S-3	The Hardest Decision I've Ever Made DM-S-3
One of the Best Decisions I've Ever Made DM-S-3	A Time I Made a Good Decision But Got a Poor Result DM-S-3
The Hardest Thing About Making Decisions Is ... DM-S-3	The Easiest Thing About Making Decisions Is ... DM-S-3
What It Takes To Be Decisive DM-S-3	A Time I Was Sure I Was Doing the Right Thing DM-S-3

DECISION MAKING

Note. From *50 Activities for Teaching Emotional Intelligence, Level III: High School* (p. 62), by D. Schilling and S. Palomares, 1999, Austin, TX: PRO-ED, Inc. Copyright 1999 by PRO-ED, Inc. Adapted with permission.

Relaxing

Objective
Group members will learn to use relaxation techniques, when needed.

Materials
Relaxing poster*; *Relaxation Technique* poster*

Procedure
1. Explain to your students that they will handle things better if they are relaxed and not anxious.
2. Using the *Relaxing* poster, model the steps: (1) Do I need to relax? (2) Sit comfortably. (3) Breathe deeply.
3. Discuss ways to tell if body language is anxious: Shoulders will be tight, breathing will be shallow, stomach will be churning.
4. Have the group tighten up muscles to see the difference between *relaxed* and *tense*. Have them relax.
5. Take the group through the steps on the *Relaxation Technique* poster.

Discussion
1. "How can relaxation help us in school?"
2. "How can relaxation help us in our relationships with others?"

Evaluation
Students demonstrate using relaxation skills and identifying situations in which they plan to use them.

251

* Also available on CD

Note. From *Getting to Know You! Social Skills Curriculum for Grades 1–3* (pp. 142–144), by D. Hanken and J. Kennedy, 1998, Minneapolis, MN: Educational Media Corporation. Copyright 1998 by Educational Media Corporation. Adapted with permission.

SELF-CARE

252

Relaxing

1. Do I need to relax?

2. Sit comfortably.

3. Breathe deeply.

Note. From *Getting to Know You! Social Skills Curriculum for Grades 1–3* (p. 144), by D. Hanken and J. Kennedy, 1998, Minneapolis, MN: Educational Media Corporation. Copyright 1998 by Educational Media Corporation. Adapted with permission.

Relaxation Technique

253

- Breathe deeply throughout relaxation.

- Get in a comfortable sitting position.

- Close your eyes, and begin to pay attention to your own breathing.

- Think only about your breath as it flows in and out of your body.

- Say to yourself : "I am relaxing, breathing smoothly and rhythmically. Fresh oxygen flows in and out of my body. I feel calm, renewed, and refreshed."

- Continue to focus on your breath as it flows in and out, thinking of nothing but the smooth, rhythmic process of your own breathing.

- After 5 minutes, stand up, stretch, smile, and continue your daily activities.

SELF-CARE

Note. From *Getting to Know You! Social Skills Curriculum for Grades 1–3* (p. 143), by D. Hanken and J. Kennedy, 1998, Minneapolis, MN: Educational Media Corporation. Copyright 1998 by Educational Media Corporation. Adapted with permission.

Affirm Your Body!

Objectives

Group members will:

1. discuss body images as a way to improve them,
2. build a more positive relationship with their physical selves,
3. celebrate their positive physical qualities, and
4. create an artistic model of their bodies.

254

Materials

Butcher paper, cut to lengths to match the students' heights; markers; scissors; glue; decorative art materials such as feathers, glitter, ribbons, sparkles, crayons

Procedure

1. Say to the group: *Many times the messages we give our bodies are quite sad. It is not uncommon to hear comments like: "I am so fat," "I am so skinny," "I am so clumsy," "I can't do anything," "I wish I could look like ...," "Why can't I be (taller, stronger, shorter, prettier)?" Comparisons to others can lead to painful feelings when we aren't happy with our physical appearance.*
2. Have students work in pairs. One will lie down on a piece of butcher paper, and the partner will trace around his or her body with a crayon. Then they will switch places.
3. Have each student decorate the outline to express himself or herself positively. "Who am I?" and "How can I positively express myself and my body in art?" are the questions.
4. When the artwork is done, ask the group members each to write three positive words about their bodies on their portrait in this format: "My body is _____, _____, and _____."
5. Ask each member to stand, holding his or her self-portraits.

Discussion

1. "How does your art show us the positive attributes of your body?"
2. "How can you feel more like the 'you' in your portrait?"
3. "Are there any thoughts you have that get in the way of feeling good about your body? What could you think instead?"

Evaluation

Students demonstrate through their artwork that they can identify positive attributes of their bodies.

SELF-CARE

Note. From *Group Activities for Kids Who Hurt* (pp. 48–49), by S. J. Blair, 2001, Austin, TX: PRO-ED, Inc. Copyright 2001 by PRO-ED, Inc. Adapted with permission.

My Body and Me

Objectives

Group members will:

1. experience the practice of self-massage,
2. practice a set of movements for stress relief,
3. become aware of the body, and
4. celebrate the self in the body.

Materials

255

None needed

Procedure

1. Have group members stand with enough space around them so that each can move comfortably. Ask the group members to close their eyes for a moment, breathe deeply, and be aware of their bodies.

2. Instruct them to open their eyes. Then begin to lead the Self-Massage.

   - *Stand up, stretch your arms in the air, and reach toward the sky.*
   - *Make fists and bring your hands down to pound the top of your head, and all around the sides and back, onto your neck. You can do it hard or gently.*
   - *Now pull on your ears from top to bottom with your fingers and thumb. How big can you stretch your ears?*
   - *Take your index fingers and rub right in front of your ears until you feel heat. Then gently play drums on your cheeks with your fingers.*
   - *Pinch the bridge of your nose, right where your glasses would sit, and then rub your temples in a circle to relax your head.*
   - *Softly make circles with two fingers on your eyes, and then press gently for a few seconds and watch your inner sky.*
   - *Hammer your mouth with your fingertips, and then open it and make sounds.*
   - *Shake out your hands as you feel that you are shaking off tension and energy.*
   - *Use the fist of your right hand to pound up and down on your left shoulder, lifting your right elbow in front of you so you can reach further down onto your back. Then use your left hand on your right shoulder. Pound up your neck at the same time.*
   - *Use your fists to pound your chest while you make Tarzan sounds.*
   - *Now take your fists to pound down your arms, first on the outside and then on the inside, several times each.*
   - *Twist and pull each finger, including your thumbs, one by one. Shake out your hands.*
   - *Pound three lines down your thighs: the center, inside, and outside.*
   - *Now lean forward and pound your back and buttocks, especially where your jean pockets would be located. It's okay to giggle.*
   - *Stand up straight again and stretch to the sky.*
   - *Bring your hands together and clap for how wonderful you are.*

SELF-CARE

SOS! *A Practical Guide*

Discussion

1. "What do you notice about your body now that is different from before you experienced Self-Massage?"
2. "If you noticed any places in your body that were tender, what messages might those places have been telling you?"
3. "Why is it important to listen to our bodies?"

Evaluation

Students demonstrate relaxation skills of self-massage and identify the benefits of using this technique.

Note. From *Group Activities for Kids Who Hurt* (pp. 44–46), by S. J. Blair, 2001, Austin, TX: PRO-ED, Inc. Copyright 2001 by PRO-ED, Inc. Adapted with permission.

SELF-CARE

The Breath of Life

Objectives

Group members will:

1. learn and practice two deep-breathing exercises, and

2. identify times when they can use breathing exercise for relaxation and renewal.

Materials

Chalkboard and chalk

257

Procedure

1. Begin by telling the students that various breathing exercises have proven effective in reducing anxiety, irritability, muscular tension, fatigue, and depression. Point out that a simple but effective method of relaxation is the practice of deep breathing.

2. On the chalkboard write the terms *thoracic breathing* and *diaphragmatic breathing*. Explain that thoracic breathing is shallow and takes place primarily in the upper part of the lungs, whereas diaphragmatic breathing is deep and emanates from the diagram. Explain: *The diaphragm is a muscle that separates the chest from the abdomen. When we breathe, the diaphragm expands and contracts. This action, though usually automatic, is subject to voluntary control. When air is inhaled, the diaphragm expands and tenses; when it is exhaled, the diaphragm relaxes. By lengthening the time we spend exhaling, we encourage full use of our lung capacity.*

3. To practice diaphragmatic breathing, have the students expand their abdomens so their stomachs rise and fall with each breath and their chest sizes remain relatively constant. Explain that this action, which will probably feel unnatural at first, provides sufficient oxygen to properly oxygenate the blood and maintain good mental and physical health.

4. Have the students stand or sit in chairs. Lead the first exercise—The Deep-Breathing Exercise:

   - *Sit up straight or stand erect, but relaxed.*

   - *Notice how you are breathing. Breathe slowly and deeply.*

   - *Close your eyes and breathe slowly through your nose. Inhale deeply so that the air fills the lower section of your lungs and your diaphragm pushes your stomach outward to make room for the air. Then, as your lower ribs and chest expand, fill the middle part of your lungs. Finally, as your chest rises slightly, fill in the upper part of the lungs. Do this in one continuous motion as you inhale.*

   - *Hold your breath for a few seconds.*

   - *Exhale slowly through your nose and mouth. As you exhale, allow all of the tensions to leave your body.*

   - *Continue to breathe deeply like this until I tell you to stop (3–5 minutes).*

   - *Gently open your eyes. Stay seated (or standing) in the same position for a few moments.*

SELF-CARE

5. For the second exercise, have the students stand away from chairs, desks, and each other. Lead the second exercise—The Windmill Breathing Exercise:

- *Stand straight with your arms extended in front of you.*
- *Inhale deeply so that the air fills the lower section of your lungs and your diaphragm pushes your stomach outward to make room for the air. Then, as your lower ribs and chest expand, fill the middle part of your lungs. Finally, as your chest rises slightly, fill the upper part of the lungs. Do this in one continuous motion as you inhale.*
- *Rotate your arms backward in a circle several times.*
- *Reverse direction and rotate your arms forward, or alternate directions like a windmill.*
- *Exhale forcefully through your mouth.*
- *Breathe several deep, purifying breaths.*

Discussion

1. "How did you feel while doing these exercises? How did you feel after you were finished?"
2. "How can we use these short exercises to help us relieve stress in school and at other times?"

Evaluation

Students demonstrate proficiency with deep-breathing techniques and identify the benefits of using these techniques.

Note. From *50 Activities for Teaching Emotional Intelligence, Level III: High School* (pp. 67–68), by D. Schilling and S. Palomares, 1999, Austin, TX: PRO-ED, Inc. Copyright 1999 by PRO-ED, Inc. Adapted with permission.

SELF-CARE

S–T–O–P That Thought

Objectives
Group members will:

1. learn a model for halting negative thinking patterns,
2. practice the model,
3. brainstorm recurring thoughts they would like to stop, and
4. decide on a specific thought pattern to S–T–O–P in daily life.

Materials
259

Copies of the *S–T–O–P That Thought* model* for each member; red construction paper; scissors; 5" × 5" cardboard model of a stop sign

Procedure
1. Lead a discussion of how thoughts can go around and around in our heads, even when we want them to stop. Give some examples of these "sticky" thoughts (I can't ... I'll never be good enough ... nobody likes me ... this hurt will never end ...). Ask for others to share examples of their own sticky thoughts.
2. Tell the students that it helps to focus on what you want your life to be like, things you like, talents you have, things you are good at, or what service you can offer.
3. Introduce the *S–T–O–P That Thought* model as a method for stopping a sticky thought process and replacing it with something more positive.
4. Pass out the *S–T–O–P That Thought* model sheets.
5. Brainstorm some sticky thoughts that might be helped by this model.
6. Practice aloud with a few examples.
7. Have each group member then cut out a red stop sign and paste the *S–T–O–P That Thought* model on it to keep as a reminder of the S–T–O–P process.

Discussion
1. "How do those sticky thoughts get stuck in our heads?"
2. "In what way does praising ourselves help to change our thinking?"
3. "What is the one and only thing we can control?"
4. "If we don't control our thinking, who else does?"
5. "How can I change my thinking to feel good about myself?"

Evaluation
Students demonstrate proficiency at stopping negative self-talk and are able to apply the technique to real-life situations.

SELF-CARE

* Also available on CD

Note. From *Group Activities for Kids Who Hurt* (pp. 21–24), by S. J. Blair, 2001, Austin, TX: PRO-ED, Inc. Copyright 2001 by PRO-ED, Inc. Adapted with permission.

260

When you have negative thinking, use this process ...

S–T–O–P That Thought

Stop when you become aware of a sticky thought.

Then rephrase the thought into more helpful words.

Over and over again, repeat the new thought.

Praise yourself for changing your thinking.

Note. From *Group Activities for Kids Who Hurt* (p. 24), by S. J. Blair, 2001, Austin, TX: PRO-ED, Inc. Copyright 2001 by PRO-ED, Inc. Adapted with permission.

SELF-CARE

The Memory Poem

Objectives

Group members will:

1. recall poignant memories,
2. reflect and write about the memories,
3. share poetry and memories, and
4. discuss the process of releasing memories.

Materials

261

Copies of the *Memory Poem* sheet* for each member; paper; pens and pencils

Procedure

1. Ask group members to reflect on things or people in their pasts that they treasure. Suggest that the memory could be about something tangible or not, but it should be something or someone who has influenced them in a real way. It might be helpful to brainstorm and jot down a list of ideas to get the process started.

2. Introduce the structure of the Memory Poem, and read examples, noting how the examples fit the format.

Memory Poem Structure

One: One or two words naming the memory
Two: Four words that describe it
Three: Where was the memory created?
Four: Why you like this thing or person
Five: Special times you shared together
Six: What happened to the person or thing
Seven: A feeling you have about this thing or person

Person Example

Free
Foster, Joyous, Chubby, Sweet
Lived with me on Delaware Street
Always gave me baby kisses
Eating sand on California coast
Moved back with her own family
Love forever

Thing Example

Ice skates
White, sharp, shining, fast
On frozen ponds in Michigan
Gift from favorite grandpa
Skated with friends and shared hot chocolate
Gave to younger cousin
Joy

SELF-CARE

3. Take a few moments to write a poem as a group about something the members have in common (e.g., school food, a beloved mascot).

4. Once the students understand the idea, have them individually reflect and write their own Memory Poems.

5. Invite the members to share poems aloud if they choose.

Discussion

1. "In what ways do we own our memories or do they own us?"

2. "What part of remembering is positive? Negative?"

3. "If we have hurtful memories, what are some ways to let them go?"

4. "How do we hold onto our happy memories?"

262

Evaluation

Students create memory poems and find positive ways to frame painful memories.

---

* Also available on CD

Note. From *Group Activities for Kids Who Hurt* (pp. 66–68), by S. J. Blair, 2001, Austin, TX: PRO-ED, Inc. Copyright 2001 by PRO-ED, Inc. Adapted with permission.

SELF-CARE

Memory Poem

_____
(One or two words recalling your memory)

_____, _____, _____, and _____
(Four words that describe your memory)

_____
(Where was the memory created?)

_____
(Why did you like this thing or person?)

_____
(Special times you shared together)

_____
(What happened to the person or thing?)

_____
(A feeling you have about this person or thing)

1. Find a friend or family member to help write a person or thing Memory Poem. You could teach him or her the pattern, and enjoy sharing ideas and the time together!

2. Do you know anyone who is experiencing a painful time right now? In what way could you reach out to that person to be kind and caring? For example, could you make a card, call him or her up, or give a surprise hug?

    Write your idea here: _____

    _____.

Make a happy face when you have been kind to someone.

SELF-CARE

Note. From _Group Activities for Kids Who Hurt_ (p. 68), by S. J. Blair, 2001, Austin, TX: PRO-ED, Inc. Copyright 2001 by PRO-ED, Inc. Adapted with permission.

Success Bombardment

Objectives
Group members will:

1. recognize and describe their own worth and worthiness,
2. identify strengths, talents, and special abilities in themselves and others, and
3. practice positive self-talk.

Materials

264

Copies of the *Success Inventory** for each member; 15 small, self-adhesive labels per student; one copy of the *Target* worksheet* for each student

Procedure

1. Distribute the *Success Inventory* sheets. Ask the students to think of successes they have had. Remind them that their lives are really a series of successes, one after another, year after year. Have the students individually fill out the sheets. If students need help getting started, help them remember learning to walk, talk, dress, dance, play, sing, count, problem solve, read, write, skateboard, play volleyball, cook, use a computer, drive a car, and so forth.

2. Give 15 small, blank labels and a *Target* worksheet to each student.

3. Direct the students to take turns describing their accomplishments to the other members of the group. *Tell the group why you picked these particular successes. After you share, the other members of the group will each make three labels that describe positive things about you based on the successes you shared. Then, while you hold up your target, one person will look directly at you, tell you what he or she has written on each label, and stick the labels on your target. Then the other members will take their turns "bombarding" you with their success labels in the same manner. The second person in the group will then take a turn. Then a third person will be the target, and so on.*

Discussion

1. "How did you feel after doing this exercise?"
2. "What did you learn about yourself? ... about other members of the group?"
3. "How did you decide which accomplishments to include on your list?"
4. "How can you use what you experienced with your positive accomplishments to help you with your goals?"

Evaluation

Students reflect on their accomplishments and use them to develop positive self-talk.

SELF-CARE

---

* Also available on CD

Note. From *Activities for Counseling Underachievers* (pp. 112–115), by J. Bleuer, S. Palomares, and G. Walz, 1993, Austin, TX: PRO-ED, Inc. Copyright 1993 by PRO-ED, Inc. Adapted with permission.

Success Inventory

Your life is a chronicle of successes, one after the other, year after year. The things you've accomplished could fill a book. Look back now at the child you were and the young adult you have become. Recall some of the many things you've learned and achieved, and write the most memorable here:

- Five skills I mastered before the age of 5 were:

    1.

    2.

    3.

    4.

    5.

- Four things I accomplished between the ages of 5 and 8 were:

    1.

    2.

    3.

    4.

- Four of my achievements between the ages of 8 and 11 were:

    1.

    2.

    3.

    4.

- Three major things I accomplished between the ages of 11 and 13 were:

    1.

    2.

    3.

- Three of my successes from the age of 13 to now are:

    1.

    2.

    3.

SELF-CARE

Note. From *Activities for Counseling Underachievers* (pp. 114–115), by J. Bleuer, S. Palomares, and G. Walz, 1993, Austin, TX: PRO-ED, Inc. Copyright 1993 by PRO-ED, Inc. Adapted with permission.

266

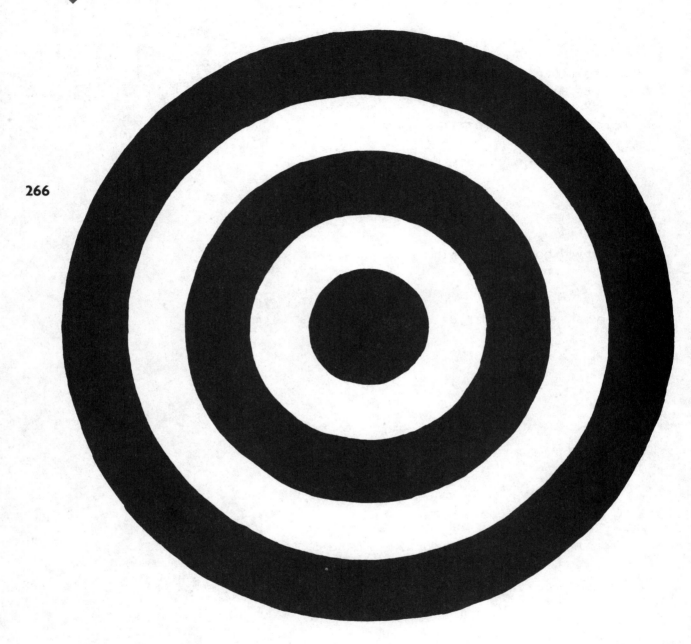

SELF-CARE

Centering and Balancing

Objectives

Group members will:

1. identify and label stressful situations associated with strong negative emotions, and

2. practice a simple meditation exercise that can be used to relieve stress and regain emotional balance.

Materials

Cassette or CD player and relaxing music

267

Procedure

1. Begin the activity by talking to the students about what it means to be out of balance. Start with bodily examples, then move the discussion toward emotions. For example, ask *Have you ever lost your balance?*

2. Tell the students that we can get out of balance on the inside, too. *One way we can get out of balance inside is from strong, negative emotions. If we get very nervous or angry or afraid, we start to feel and act "out of control" or "unbalanced." To get back in balance, we have to become centered again. "Being centered inside" means being quiet, calm, relaxed, and alert. Today we're going to practice a simple exercise that will help us become centered.*

3. Play music and lead the students in a meditation exercise.

Simple Meditation

Tell the students to sit comfortably and close their eyes. Then, slowly read this centering exercise in a soothing tone:

> *Take several deep breaths ... Feel your body begin to relax ... Breathe in and hold it ... Breathe out ... Breathe in and hold it ... Breathe out ... Focus your attention on your feet ... Breathe in so deeply that you can feel the air move through your body ... all the way to your toes ... Do that again ... This time, feel the air sweeping away all the tension and negative feelings with it ... Breathe out ... releasing the tension ... pushing out the negative feelings ... Feel your body relax more and more with each breath ... Feel your stomach relax ... your heart ... your chest ... your shoulders ... Keep breathing ... deeply ... until all of the tension has left your body ... Then, when you are ready, bring your awareness back to this room and open your eyes.*

Discussion

1. "How did you feel when you were doing the relaxation exercise? How did you feel immediately afterwards?"

2. "Why is it important to stay in balance, or get back in balance when you are stressed?"

3. "When you feel stressed or upset, what happens to your ability to study and learn?"

4. "How might you use this exercise on your own, at school, or at home?"

SELF-CARE

Evaluation

Students learn a simple meditation exercise and develop techniques for meditation they can use on their own.

268

Note. From *50 Activities for Teaching Emotional Intelligence, Level II: Middle School* (pp. 67–67), by D. Schilling and S. Palomares, 1996, Austin, TX: PRO-ED, Inc. Copyright 1996 by PRO-ED, Inc. Adapted with permission.

SELF-CARE

Effectively Managing Time

Objectives

Group members will:

1. keep track of their time use for one week, and

2. identify specific ways of organizing their time and surroundings.

Materials

Chart paper; markers; masking tape; a copy of *Keeping a Time Log* sheet* and *Time Management Tips* for each student

269

Procedure

1. Say to the group, *By following a few simple rules and acquiring good time management habits, you can accomplish more and have time for yourself, too. Time management helps you get things done on time so you can avoid last-minute rush jobs and the feeling of being unprepared. By planning your activities at school, home, and work, you'll get the most out of each day and you won't feel like you've wasted the time you do have.*

2. Discuss key strategies for time management:

   Strategy 1: Organize Your Time

   - Keep a planning calendar.
   - Record all the things you must do.
   - Check your calendar first thing every morning.

   Strategy 2: Prioritize Your Activities

   - Decide what's most important, second most important, and so on.
   - Do the most important things first.

   Strategy 3: Organize Your Home Environment

   - Have a place to study and a surface (or computer) to write on.
   - Reduce or eliminate distractions.
   - Keep materials and equipment handy.

   Strategy 4: Organize Your School Environment

   - Keep an orderly locker, backpack, and notebook.
   - Hold a clean-up, throw-out, and get-organized session each night.
   - Make sure you have all supplies and assignments ready for the next day.

3. Distribute *Keeping a Time Log* sheets. Go over the codes and directions.

4. Review and discuss *Time Management Tips*. Ask the group members to bring their completed time logs to the next session.

Discussion

1. "How satisfied are you with your use of time?"

2. "Where do you most need to get organized?"

3. "How can you reduce or eliminate wasted time?"

SELF-CARE

SOS! *A Practical Guide*

Evaluation

Students learn time management tips and apply them to their time log to be better organized and eliminate wasted time.

Note. From *Group Activities for Counselors* (pp. 114–117), by S. Elliot, 1994, Austin, TX: PRO-ED, Inc. Copyright 1994 by PRO-ED, Inc. Adapted with permission.

SELF-CARE

Keeping a Time Log

Directions: Keep track of your time for 1 week. Every day, in each square of the log, write the code that stands for the activity you did during that time period. Make up your own codes for activities that are not listed.

CODES:

CL:	Class time	FR:	Time with friends	TE:	Telephone
FM:	Family activity	ST:	Studying	TV:	Television
HO:	Hobby	SH:	Shopping	TR:	Traveling to and from
ET:	Eating	SL:	Sleeping	CH:	Chores
		SP:	Sports	RE:	Relaxing

271

Time	Monday	Tuesday	Wednesday	Thursday	Friday	Saturday	Sunday
6 AM							
7 AM							
8 AM							
9 AM							
10 AM							
11 AM							
12 PM							
1 PM							
2 PM							
3 PM							
4 PM							
5 PM							
6 PM							
7 PM							
8 PM							
9 PM							
10 PM							
11 PM							

SELF-CARE

Note. From *Group Activities for Counselors* (p. 116), by S. Elliot, 1994, Austin, TX: PRO-ED, Inc. Copyright 1994 by PRO-ED, Inc. Adapted with permission.

SOS! *A Practical Guide*

Time Management Tips

1. **Learn to say "no."** If someone wants you to do something that you aren't interested in doing, it is okay to turn down the offer. In the same way, assert your rights when someone is wasting *your* time. You have the right to make good use of your time and energy. Do things that you benefit from and really enjoy. Spend time with people who add to your life.

2. **Make decisions.** Low energy and confusion sometimes result from failing to act when decisions need to be made. By making decisions and following through, you spend your time on important tasks instead of wasting it on worry or confusion.

3. **Look ahead and set goals.** Everyone should have short-term and long-range goals. You can set goals as far ahead as you choose. Stay flexible but start preparing now for the future.

4. **Get your body and mind in shape.** Budget some time for exercise and make sure you eat right and get enough sleep. When you feel rushed or stressed during the day, take a break and relax.

5. **Tackle the toughest part of any job or assignment first.** Don't start with the easy stuff. Take advantage of your freshness and enthusiasm when you first begin work. Accomplishing the tough part will spur you on to complete the rest of the task.

6. **Don't put things off.** Procrastination is the biggest obstacle between you and increased effectiveness. Start now and take each project one step at a time. Keep moving and strive to eliminate procrastination from your life.

7. **Be flexible.** Things are always changing. Be willing to adapt and switch directions if new circumstances or information arise. Be open to new possibilities.

Note. From *Group Activities for Counselors* (p. 117), by S. Elliot, 1994, Austin, TX: PRO-ED, Inc. Copyright 1994 by PRO-ED, Inc. Adapted with permission.

SOS! *A Practical Guide*

SELF-CARE

References

Beane, A. L. (1999). *Bully free classroom*. Minneapolis, MN: Free Spirit.

Berg, I. K., & Steiner, T. (2003). *Children's solution work*. New York: Norton.

Bertolino, B., & Schultheis, G. (2002). *The therapist's notebook for families: Solution-oriented exercises for working with parents, children, and adolescents*. Binghamton, NY: Haworth Clinical Practice Press.

Blair, S. J. (2001). *Group activities for kids who hurt*. Austin, TX: PRO-ED.

Bleuer, J., Palomares, S., & Walz, G. (1993). *Activities for counseling underachievers*. Austin, TX: PRO-ED.

Borba, M. (1989). *Esteem builders*. Austin, TX: PRO-ED.

Brigman, G., & Early, B. (1991). *Group counseling for school counselors*. Portland, ME: J. Weston Walch.

Brown, N. (2004). *Psychoeducational groups* (2nd ed.). New York: Brunner-Routledge.

Campbell, C. A., & Dahir, C. A. (1997). *Sharing the vision: National standards for school counseling programs*. Alexandria, VA: American School Counselor Association.

Dennison, S. T. (1997). *Creating positive support groups for at-risk children: Ten complete curriculums for the most common problems among elementary students, grades 1–8*. Austin, TX: PRO-ED.

Devencenzi, J., & Pendergast, S. (1999). *Belonging: Self and social discovery for children and adolescents*. Austin, TX: PRO-ED.

Elliot, S. (1994). *Group activities for counselors*. Austin, TX: PRO-ED.

Gajewski, N. (1993). *Social star*. Eau Clair, WI: Thinking Publications.

Gladding, S. T. (2003). *Group work: A counseling specialty*. Upper Saddle River, NJ: Merrill/Prentice-Hall.

Greenberg, K. R. (2003). Group counseling in K–12 schools. Boston: Allyn & Bacon.

Hanken, D., & Kennedy, J. (1998). *Getting to know you! Social skills curriculum for grades 1–3*. Minneapolis, MN: Educational Media.

Huggins, P. (1998). *Helping kids handle anger*. Longmont, CO: Sopris West.

Jackson, T. (1995). *More activities that teach*. Cedar City, UT: Red Rock.

Kymissis, P., & Halperin, D. (Eds.). (1996). *Group therapy with children and adolescents*. Washington, DC: American Psychiatric Press.

Landy, L. (1990). *Child support through small group counseling*. Indianapolis, IN: KIDRIGHTS.

Loesch, L. C., & Ritchie, M. H. (2005). *The accountable school counselor*. Austin, TX: PRO-ED.

Malekoff, A. (2004). *Group work with adolescents: Principles and practice* (2nd ed.). New York: Guilford Press.

Marmar, C., Horowitz, M., Weiss, D., & Marziali, E. (1986). The development of the Therapeutic Alliance Rating System. In L. Greenberg & W. Pinsof (Eds.), *The psychotherapeutic process: A research handbook* (pp. 367–390). New York: Guilford Press.

Masterson, J. F. (1988). *The search for the real self: Unmasking the personality disorders of our age*. New York: Simon & Schuster.

Metcalf, L. (1997). *Parenting toward solutions: How parents can use skills they already have to raise responsible, loving kids.* Paramus, NJ: Prentice Hall.

Metcalf, L. (2002). *Counseling toward solutions: A practical solution-focused program for working with students, teachers, and parents* (2nd ed.). San Francisco: Jossey-Bass.

Murphy, J. J. (1997). *Solution-focused counseling in middle and high schools.* Alexandria, VA: American Counseling Association.

O'Hanlon, B. (1999). *Do one thing different: Ten simple ways to change your life.* New York: HarperCollins.

O'Hanlon, B., & Beadle, S. (1997). *A guide to possibility land: Fifty-one methods for doing brief, respectful therapy.* New York: Norton.

Orlinsky, D. E., Grawe, K., & Parks, B. K. (1994). Process and outcome in psychotherapy: Noch einmal. In A. E. Bergin & S. L. Garfield (Eds.), *Handbook of psychotherapy and behavior change* (4th ed., pp. 270–376). New York: Wiley.

Ormont, L. (1992). *The group therapy experience.* New York: St. Martin's Press.

Palomares, S., Schuster, S., & Watkins, C. (1992). *The sharing circle handbook.* Austin, TX: PRO-ED.

Pichot, T., & Dolan, Y. M. (2003). *Solution-focused brief therapy: Its effective use in agency settings.* Binghampton, NY: Haworth Clinical Practice Press.

Rogala, J. A., Lambert, R., & Verhage, K. (1992). *Developmental guidance classroom activities for use with National Career Development Guidelines, grades 10–12.* Madison, WI: Center on Education and Work.

Rowling, J. K. *Harry Potter and the sorcerer's stone.* New York: Scholastic Press.

Rutan, S., & Stone, W. (2001). *Psychodynamic group psychotherapy* (3rd ed.). New York: Guilford Press.

Schilling, D., & Palomares, S. (1996). *50 activities for teaching emotional intelligence, level II: Middle school.* Austin, TX: PRO-ED.

Schilling, D., & Palomares, S. (1999). *50 activities for teaching emotional intelligence, level I: Elementary school.* Austin, TX: PRO-ED.

Schilling, D., & Palomares, S. (1999). *50 activities for teaching emotional intelligence, level III: High school.* Austin, TX: PRO-ED.

Schilling, D., Schwallie-Giddis, P., & Giddis, W. J. (1995). *Preparing teens for the world of work.* Austin, TX: PRO-ED.

Sklare, G. B. (2005). *Brief counseling that works: A solution-focused approach for school counselors and administrators* (2nd ed.). Thousand Oaks, CA: Corwin Press.

Swanson, A. J. (1996). Children in groups: Indications and contexts. In P. Kymissis & D. A. Halperin (Eds.), *Group therapy with children and adolescents.* Washington, DC: American Psychiatric Press.

Vernon, A. (1989). *Thinking, feeling, behaving: Grades 1–6.* Champaign, IL: Research Press.

Vernon, A. (1989). *Thinking, feeling, behaving: Grades 7–12.* Champaign, IL: Research Press.

Webb, W. (1999). *Solutioning: Solution-focused interventions for counselors.* Philadelphia: Taylor & Francis Group.

Whiston, S., & Sexton, T. (1998). A review of school counseling outcome research: Implications for practice. *Journal of Counseling and Development, 76,* 412–426.

Wild, J. D. (1963). *Existence and the world of freedom.* Englewood Cliffs, NJ: Prentice Hall.

Winnicott, D. W. (1971). Letter to Mme. Jeannine Kalamovitch. Nouvelle revue de psychoanalyse (Vol. 3). Quoted by M. Kahn in *Introduction to Winnicott's collected papers* (2nd ed.). Toronto: Clarke, Irwin, 1975.

Yalom, I., & Leszcz, M. (2005). *The theory and practice of group psychotherapy* (5th ed.). New York: Basic Books.

About the Authors

Patricia K. Tollison, PhD, has taught at the preschool, middle school, and university levels and has served as support staff, providing assessment and consultation for teachers and parents. She is currently a psychologist in private practice in Austin, Texas. She is a clinical member of American Group Psychotherapy Association, a certified group psychotherapist, and a past president of Austin Group Psychotherapy Society.

Katherine O. Synatschk, PhD, LPC, has been the director of counseling for a large urban school district, a school counselor, a school social worker, a special education teacher, and a counselor educator. She trains and consults on counseling issues at the local, state, national, and international levels. She is currently adjunct professor at Texas State University and the Executive Editor of Books and Materials at PRO-ED, Inc.